Explore and Learn

Earth and Space

World Book, Inc.
233 N. Michigan Avenue
Chicago, IL 60601
U.S.A.

Volume 1: Earth and Space
Volume 2: Science and Technology
Volume 3: The Natural World
Volume 4: People in Place and Time
Volume 5: Me and My Body
Volume 6: Atlas of the World

For information about other World Book publications, visit our Web site at **http://www.worldbookonline.com** or call **1-800-WORLDBK (967-5325)**.

For information about sales to schools and libraries,
call **1-800-975-3250 (United States); 1-800-837-5365 (Canada)**.

Library of Congress Cataloging-in-Publication Data

Explore and learn--Earth and space.
    p. cm.
    Summary: "Introduction to Earth and space, using simple text, stories, illustrations, and photos. Features include activities and projects, definitions, review questions, fun facts, school curriculum correlations, and an index"--Provided by publisher.
    Includes index.
    ISBN 978-0-7166-3017-3
    1. Astronomy--Juvenile literature. 2. Outer space--Juvenile literature. 3. Earth--Juvenile literature. I. World Book, Inc.
II. Title: Earth and space.
QB46.E95 2008
520--dc22
                    2008001353

Explore and Learn
Set ISBN: 978-0-7166-3016-6

Printed in China
1 2 3 4 5 12 11 10 09 08

NASA/ESA/Hubble Heritage Team
(STScI/AURA); © Photographers Choice
RF/SuperStock

Editor in Chief: Paul A. Kobasa

Supplementary Publications
 Associate Director: Scott Thomas
 Managing Editor: Barbara A. Mayes
 Senior Editor: Kristina Vaicikonis
 Manager, Research: Cheryl Graham

Manager, Editorial Operations (Rights & Permissions): Loranne K. Shields

Graphics and Design
 Associate Director: Sandra M. Dyrlund
 Associate Manager, Design: Brenda B. Tropinski
 Associate Manager, Photography: Tom Evans
 Coordinator: Matt Carrington

Production
 Director, Manufacturing and Pre-Press: Carma Fazio
 Manager, Manufacturing: Steven Hueppchen
 Production Technology Manager: Anne Fritzinger
 Proofreader: Emilie Schrage

Marketing
 Chief Marketing Officer: Patricia Ginnis
 Associate Director: Jennifer Parello

Specialist consultants: Dr. Belinda Ashon; Clive Carpenter; Janet Dyson MEd (education consultant); Tim Furniss (spaceflight journalist and author); Elysa Jacobs; Keith Lye BA, FRGS (geographical author and consultant); Steve Parker BSc (Scientific Fellow of the Zoological Society of London); Peter Riley Bsc, Cbiol, MIBiol, PGCE (science writer and consultant); Sue Robson MA, PGCE (Senior Lecturer in education); Carol Watson (children's author)

Explore and Learn

Earth and Space

volume 1

WORLD
BOOK

a Scott Fetzer company
Chicago

www.worldbookonline.com

Contents

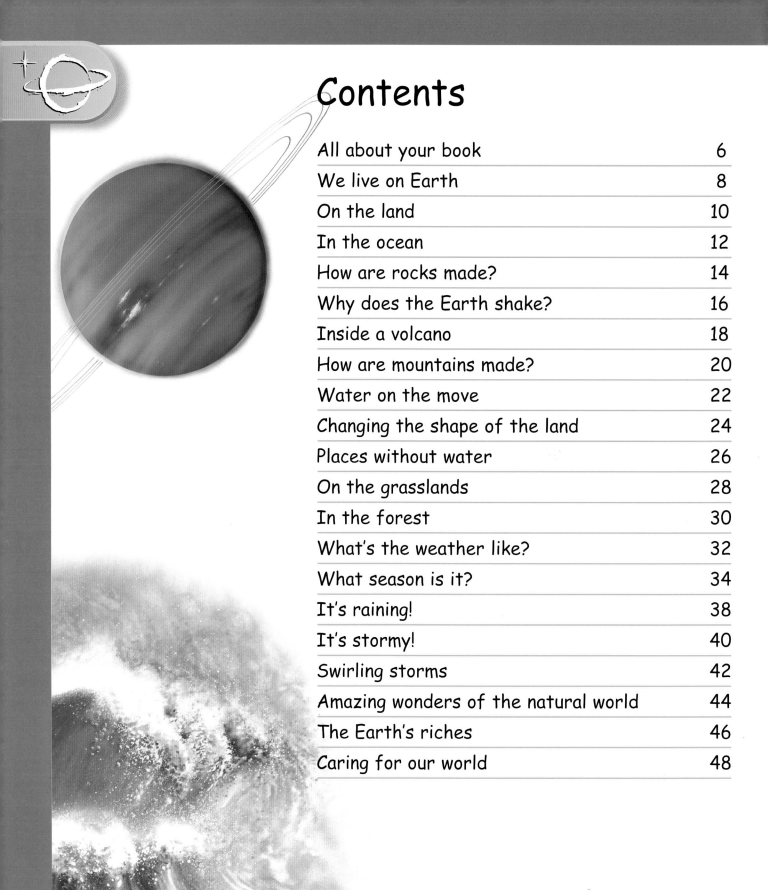

All about your book	6
We live on Earth	8
On the land	10
In the ocean	12
How are rocks made?	14
Why does the Earth shake?	16
Inside a volcano	18
How are mountains made?	20
Water on the move	22
Changing the shape of the land	24
Places without water	26
On the grasslands	28
In the forest	30
What's the weather like?	32
What season is it?	34
It's raining!	38
It's stormy!	40
Swirling storms	42
Amazing wonders of the natural world	44
The Earth's riches	46
Caring for our world	48

Our planet Earth 50

What is the Sun? 52

The Sun's family 54

Around the Sun 56

The Earth and the Moon 58

Does the Moon change shape? 60

The rocky planets 62

Giant balls of gas 64

Faraway planets 66

Bits and pieces in space 68

Three, two, one... lift-off! 70

Traveling into space 72

Journey to the Moon 74

What's in space? 76

Inside a space station 78

Is anyone there? 82

Watching the stars 84

Millions and millions of stars 86

Deep into space 88

Can you remember? 90

Index 92

All about your book

Explore and Learn will take you on a journey of discovery. Its six volumes will lead you through the world of plants and animals, into science and technology, explaining how things work and why. It will tell you about the world you live in, traveling farther into space and beyond. You can discover new and wonderful things about yourself and how you communicate with those around you.

Thumb index This is a guide to what each page contains. If you turn the pages quickly you will easily be able to find the subjects you are interested in.

Volume button This tells you which volume you are looking at. Here is the Earth and Space button that explores our world.

exploring

Think, find, research, act out – these boxes help you to discover more about what you have read on a page. See if your family and friends can help you with some of these activities and ideas.

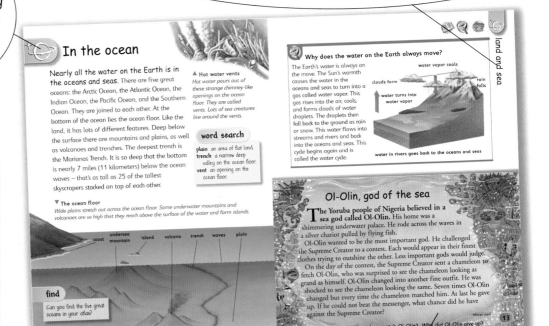

In the ocean

Nearly all the water on the Earth is in the oceans and seas. There are five great oceans: the Arctic Ocean, the Atlantic Ocean, the Indian Ocean, the Pacific Ocean, and the Southern Ocean. They are joined to each other. At the bottom of the ocean lies the ocean floor. Like the land, it has lots of different features. Deep below the surface there are mountains and plains, as well as volcanoes and trenches. The deepest trench is the Marianas Trench. It is so deep that the bottom is nearly 7 miles (11 kilometers) below the ocean waves – that's as tall as 25 of the tallest skyscrapers stacked on top of each other.

▲ **Hot water vents** Hot water pours out of these strange chimney-like openings on the ocean floor. They are called vents. Lots of sea creatures live around the vents.

word search

plain an area of flat land.
trench a narrow deep valley on the ocean floor.
vent an opening on the ocean floor.

▼ **The ocean floor** Wide plains stretch out across the ocean floor. Some underwater mountains and volcanoes are so high that they reach above the surface of the water and form islands.

coast | undersea mountain | island | volcano | trench | waves | plain

find Can you find the five great oceans in your atlas?

12

Why does the water on the Earth always move?

The Earth's water is always on the move. The Sun's warmth causes the water in the oceans and seas to turn into a gas called water vapor. This gas rises into the air, cools, and forms clouds of water droplets. The droplets then fall back to the ground as rain or snow. This water flows into streams and rivers and back into the oceans and seas. This cycle begins again and is called the water cycle.

water vapor cools
clouds form
rain falls
water turns into water vapor
water in rivers goes back to the oceans and seas

Ol-Olin, god of the sea

The Yoruba people of Nigeria believed in a sea god called Ol-Olin. His home was a shimmering underwater palace. He rode across the waves in a silver chariot pulled by flying fish.

Ol-Olin wanted to be the most important god. He challenged the Supreme Creator to a contest. Each would appear in their finest clothes trying to outshine the other. Less important gods would judge.

On the day of the contest, the Supreme Creator sent a chameleon to fetch Ol-Olin, who was surprised to see the chameleon looking as grand as himself. Ol-Olin changed into another fine outfit. He was shocked to see the chameleon looking the same. Seven times Ol-Olin changed but every time the chameleon matched him. At last he gave up. If he could not beat the messenger, what chance did he have against the Supreme Creator?

How did the chameleon match Ol-Olin? Why did Ol-Olin give up?

13

land and sea

You might choose to read each book from beginning to end, or you might decide to look up things that interest you in the index which appears at the end of each book. All the different features have been created to help you learn, discover, and have fun finding out. You might just enjoy turning each page and looking at all the wonderful pictures showing life and the world around you.

Stories You can find stories that come from different countries all over the world. Some are myths, others are fables, and some are taken from the Bible. How much can you remember? See if you can answer the questions that appear at the end of each story.

Fun facts Amazing true facts that will surprise you and your friends.

English

Maths

Science

History

Geography

Art

Music

Design and technology

Information technology

Curriculum buttons These help you, your parents, and maybe your teacher, to figure out which subjects are covered on each page. Do you like history? If so, you can turn the pages and read about history wherever you see this button. Or, maybe you like to draw – watch for this icon. Do you enjoy reading? Watch for the English button.

all about your book

Fun characters
Meet our fun characters and their dog. You will find them on our bulletin boards where we put words and pictures for you to learn. You can also find them on the **Fun facts**.

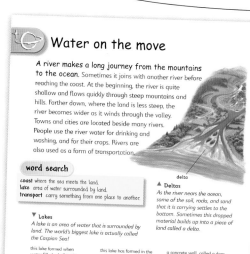

Water on the move
A river makes a long journey from the mountains to the ocean. Sometimes it joins with another river before reaching the coast. At the beginning, the river is quite shallow and flows quickly through steep mountains and hills. Farther down, where the land is less steep, the river becomes wider as it winds through the valley. Towns and cities are located beside many rivers. People use the river water for drinking and washing, and for their crops. Rivers are also used as a form of transportation.

word search
coast where the sea meets the land.
lake area of water surrounded by land.
transport carry something from one place to another.

delta

▲ **Deltas**
As the river nears the ocean, some of the soil, rocks, and sand that it is carrying settles to the bottom. Sometimes this dropped material builds up into a piece of land called a delta.

▼ **Lakes**
A lake is an area of water that is surrounded by land. The world's biggest lake is actually called the Caspian Sea!

this lake formed when water filled a hollow in the rocky land

this lake has formed in the crater of a sleeping volcano

a concrete wall, called a dam, has been built across a river to create this lake

rivers and lakes

research
What is the name of the river that runs closest to where you live? Can you find out where the river starts and ends?

22 The longest river, the Nile, flows for more than 4,100 miles (6,600 kilometers).

lake waterfall valley river mouth river stream bend 23

word search
This will explain and give the meaning of any new or difficult words that are used on a page. You can test yourself to see if you can spell the words or know what they mean. Or, see if you can find where they appear on the page.

What is the answer?
Do you know? Read on and find out. These boxes will help you learn more about history, geography, science, and other subjects. A **curriculum button** appears at the top beside the question. This tells you what subject is covered. You can choose whatever boxes you are most interested in to read about.

Projects
You can draw, paint, build, and construct all sorts of different things. You will find a list of everything you will need to make each project. Carefully follow the step-by-step instructions that tell you how to make and complete each project. Don't forget to ask an adult for help with some of the more difficult steps.

Stellar constellation
You will need
- glow-in-the-dark self-hardening clay · star-shaped cookie cutter
- rolling pin · double-sided tape
- cookie sheet

Lie in bed at night and look at the stars. Make your own glow-in-the-dark stars from self-hardening clay.

● Roll the clay out on a clean surface. Using a star-shaped cookie cutter, cut out small stars.

● Harden them according to the manufacturer's instructions, then ask an adult to attach them to your ceiling or wall with double-sided tape.

Always wash your hands after using self-hardening clay.

87

Children should be assisted in using certain tools and undertaking particular tasks. Children should not be left unsupervised to carry out these projects.

We live on Earth

Where do you live? Wherever it is — it's on Earth. The Earth is a huge rocky ball that spins slowly around and around. Parts of the Earth are covered with land. Other parts are covered with huge areas of water called oceans. The whole Earth is surrounded by a layer of air. There are living things in nearly every part of the Earth — on the land, in the water, and in the air. The warmth and light from the Sun make it possible for all these living things to stay alive.

▲ **Ice deserts**
Ice deserts are so cold that very few kinds of plants can grow there and only the tiniest animals can live there.

▼ **Hot deserts**
Hot deserts are areas of hot, dry land.

▲ **Forests**
Forests cover large areas of the land.

▼ **Mountains**
Some of the land is covered with high rocky mountains.

word search

plankton very tiny plants and animals that float in the ocean.

▼ Life on Earth
Animals and plants on the Earth need the Sun's warmth and light.

▲ Valleys
Rivers flow across the land, passing through valleys.

► Ocean life
The blue waters of the oceans are filled with living things, from very tiny plankton to enormous blue whales. Water covers about three-quarters of the Earth's surface.

think

What do living things need to stay alive on the Earth?

9

A passsenger jet takes almost two days and nights to fly once around the Earth.

On the land

Land covers over one-quarter of the surface of the Earth. The seven largest areas of land are called continents. You can find their names on the map opposite. A long time ago, all these continents were joined together to make one huge piece of land. It was called a super-continent. Very slowly, over millions of years, this super-continent broke apart to make the seven continents that we have today. The smaller areas of land that broke off became islands surrounded by water.

word search

continent one of seven very large areas of land on the Earth.
island a smaller area of land with water all the way around it.

▼ **Different types of land**
The land on the Earth's surface is covered with many different kinds of features.

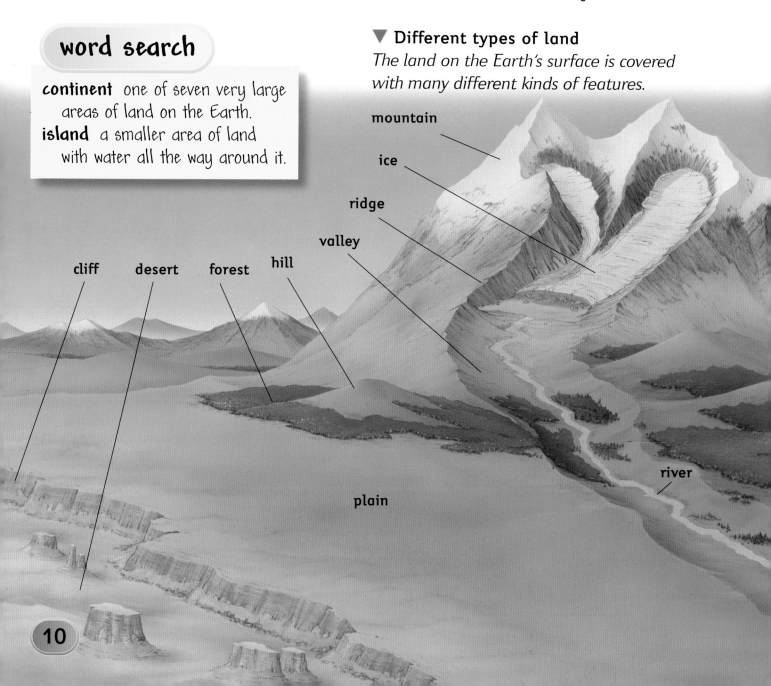

mountain

ice

ridge

valley

hill

cliff   desert   forest

plain

river

▲ Islands
All islands, whatever their shape and size, are surrounded by water.

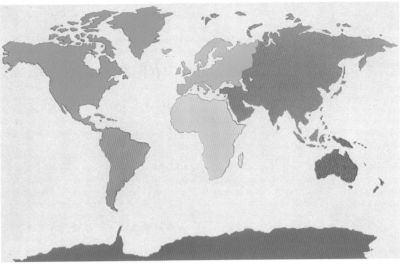

Africa ● Antarctica ● Europe ● Oceania
● North America ● Asia ● South America

▲ Seven continents
This map of the world shows the name and area of each of the world's seven continents.

▼ Earth from space
This photograph of the Earth was taken from space. Can you see the continents of North America and South America?

think
On which of the seven continents do you live?

Why do some animals live only in one place?

Madagascar is the fourth-largest island in the world. A long time ago it was joined onto the east coast of Africa. Then it broke off and drifted away. When this happened, the animals and plants on Madagascar were cut off from the ones living in Africa. The animals best suited to life on the island survived, and now many of them, like the aye-aye, live only in Madagascar and nowhere else in the world.

aye-aye

In the ocean

Nearly all the water on the Earth is in the oceans and seas. There are five great oceans: the Arctic Ocean, the Atlantic Ocean, the Indian Ocean, the Pacific Ocean, and the Southern Ocean. They are joined to each other. At the bottom of the ocean lies the ocean floor. Like the land, it has lots of different features. Deep below the surface there are mountains and plains, as well as volcanoes and trenches. The deepest trench is the Marianas Trench. It is so deep that the bottom is nearly 7 miles (11 kilometers) below the ocean waves — that's as tall as 25 of the tallest skyscrapers stacked on top of each other.

▲ **Hot water vents**
Hot water pours out of these strange chimney-like openings on the ocean floor. They are called vents. Lots of sea creatures live around the vents.

word search

plain an area of flat land.
trench a narrow deep valley on the ocean floor.
vent an opening on the ocean floor.

▼ **The ocean floor**
Wide plains stretch out across the ocean floor. Some underwater mountains and volcanoes are so high that they reach above the surface of the water and form islands.

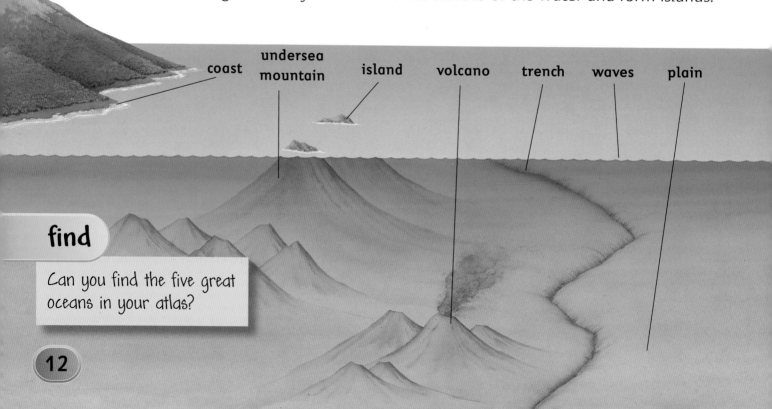

coast   undersea mountain   island   volcano   trench   waves   plain

find

Can you find the five great oceans in your atlas?

Why does the water on the Earth always move?

The Earth's water is always on the move. The Sun's warmth causes the water in the oceans and seas to turn into a gas called water vapor. This gas rises into the air, cools, and forms clouds of water droplets. The droplets then fall back to the ground as rain or snow. This water flows into streams and rivers and back into the oceans and seas. This cycle begins again and is called the water cycle.

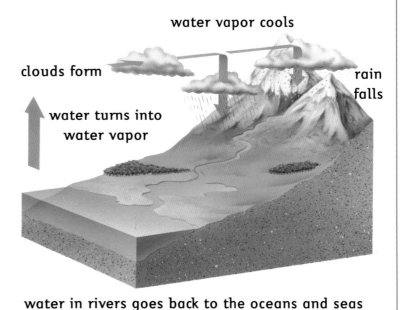

water vapor cools

clouds form

rain falls

water turns into water vapor

water in rivers goes back to the oceans and seas

Ol-Olin, god of the sea

The Yoruba people of Nigeria believed in a sea god called Ol-Olin. His home was a shimmering underwater palace. He rode across the waves in a silver chariot pulled by flying fish.

Ol-Olin wanted to be the most important god. He challenged the Supreme Creator to a contest. Each would appear in their finest clothes trying to outshine the other. Less important gods would judge.

On the day of the contest, the Supreme Creator sent a chameleon to fetch Ol-Olin, who was surprised to see the chameleon looking as grand as himself. Ol-Olin changed into another fine outfit. He was shocked to see the chameleon looking the same. Seven times Ol-Olin changed but every time the chameleon matched him. At last he gave up. If he could not beat the messenger, what chance did he have against the Supreme Creator?

African myth

13

How did the chameleon match Ol-Olin? Why did Ol-Olin give up?

How are rocks made?

Rocks are the hard parts of the Earth's surface. They can be seen in mountains, hills, and cliffs by the ocean. Other rocks are hidden under soil, water, or ice. There are three main kinds of rock. Igneous rock is made from the hot liquid that erupts inside volcanoes. Sedimentary rock is made from sand, mud, pieces of older rocks, or from the skeletons and shells of animals that lived long ago. Metamorphic rock has been changed by heat, or by heat and pressure together.

ammonite dies

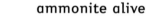

ammonite alive

word search

fossil the hard remains of a plant or animal from long ago.
gem a beautiful and rare material often used to make jewelry.
pressure a pushing or squeezing force.

▶ **Precious stones**
Valuable gems like diamonds and emeralds are found inside some rocks.

▼ **How are rocks formed?**
The three main kinds of rock are formed in different ways.

igneous rock
melted rock cools and becomes hard

sedimentary rock
layers of mud, sand, and animal remains slowly turn into rock

metamorphic rock
rock is changed by pressure and heat

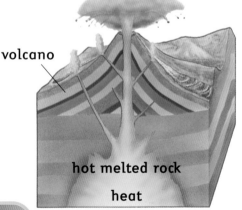

volcano

hot melted rock

heat

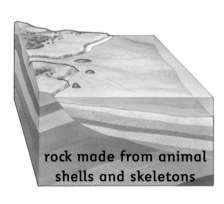

rock made from animal shells and skeletons

pressure

▼ How are fossils made?

When the remains of dead plants or animals turn into rock, we call them fossils. They tell us what living things looked like long ago. This is a fossil of an ammonite, a creature that lived in the ocean millions of years ago.

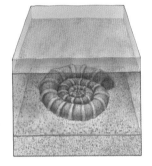

shell covered in sand

shell and sand form rock

rock splits open to show fossil

explain

How do sea creatures help to make rocks?

▶ Different rocks
Here are some different kinds of rock.

sandstone

marble

schist   shale   basalt   granite

Fossils in a few days

Fossils take millions of years to form, but you can make your own in just a few days. If you enjoy doing this, you can start your own fossil collection.

You will need
- ready-mixed plaster
- petroleum jelly
- plastic container, large enough to hold the shell
- seashell

1 Fill the container with ready-mixed plaster until it is two-thirds full. Press the shell gently into the plaster. Let it harden for 24 hours.

2 Spread petroleum jelly over the shell. Top up the container with plaster. Let it harden for 24 hours. Remove the hardened plaster from the container. Knock firmly to break apart to reveal your fossil.

Remember to wash your hands immediately after using the plaster.

Make a selection of fossils to display in your bedroom.

Why does the Earth shake?

The Earth's surface seems solid and still. But sometimes it shakes and big cracks appear. Houses and buildings topple and bridges and roads collapse. When this happens, an earthquake is taking place. Earthquakes are very powerful and can cause serious damage – they may even kill people. An earthquake happens when the rocks below the surface move suddenly and violently, often banging into each other. Some parts of the world have a lot of earthquakes. Scientists who study rocks try to work out when and where the next earthquake will happen.

2

◀ **Damage to a city**
In 1995 an earthquake caused damage to the city of Kobe, in Japan.

◀ **Earthquake waves**
Earthquakes that happen under the sea can create huge waves. The waves race toward the shore at great speed.

16

1 earthquake starts here

2 waves of energy build up

3 cracks appear in ground

4 fire breaks out

5 buildings are damaged

6 bridges collapse

design

Make a poster that shows people the dangers of earthquakes.

▲ **How an earthquake starts**

An earthquake starts in the rocks below the ground. It releases lots of energy that travels through the rocks and up to the surface.

▶ **Safe buildings**

This building in the United States has been specially designed to stand up to earthquakes. Thick columns of steel and concrete support its strong triangle-shaped frame. It is in the center of San Francisco, a city that has had many earthquakes.

word search

earthquake a violent shaking of the ground.

energy a source of power like heat and light that travels through the Earth.

release to give off.

One million earthquakes can occur in a year, but most are too tiny to be felt.

Inside a volcano

Some volcanoes are mountains or hills that can blast out clouds of dust, ash, and red-hot melted rocks. When this happens, the volcano is erupting. The fiery rocks come from deep inside the ground. They pour out of an opening at the top and run down the volcano's sides as streams of red-hot lava. When it cools, the runny lava becomes hard and turns back into rock.

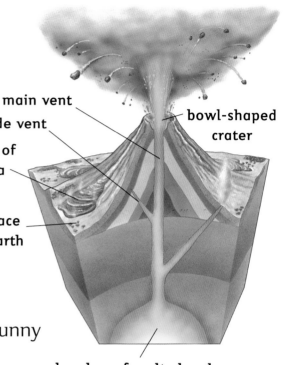

main vent
side vent
flow of lava
surface of Earth
bowl-shaped crater
chamber of melted rock

read

Look back to the page on rocks and find out more about how rocks are formed by volcanoes.

▼ **Red-hot lava**
An erupting volcano is an amazing sight. Streams of red-hot lava shoot up into the air and rush down its sides.

▲ **Eruption of a volcano**
When a volcano erupts, the melted rock rises inside the volcano and pours out through an opening called a vent.

word search

crater a bowl shape that forms at the top of a volcano.
lava red-hot melted rocks that burst out of a volcano.

18

Erupting volcano

When a volcano erupts, the lava that flows down its slopes can bury whole villages.
Build your own volcano and watch what happens when it erupts.

Before making your volcano, build some houses of modeling clay and stick them onto the mountain.

You will need

- plastic bottle, about 8 in (20 cm) high
- sheets of newspaper
- tray 14 x 20 in (35 x 50 cm)
- watered-down glue and brush
- paint and paintbrush
- half a cup of white vinegar
- two teaspoons of red food coloring
- six tablespoons of bicarbonate of soda
- modeling clay
- plastic funnel

1 Glue the base of the bottle to the center of the tray. Arrange balls of scrunched-up newspaper around the bottle. Paint glue over three sheets of newspaper and wrap them over the newspaper mountain. Make sure the top of the bottle isn't covered. When the glue has dried, paint the model.

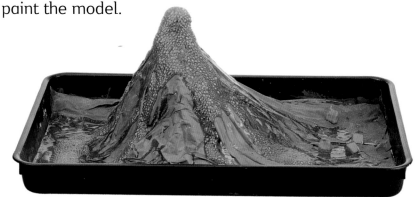

2 Now your volcano is ready to erupt. Pour the bicarbonate of soda through the funnel into the bottle. Add food coloring to the vinegar, then pour it into the bottle using the funnel. Now watch the lava edge its way over the tip of the volcano and down its slopes.

Why do volcanoes erupt?

When you mix bicarbonate of soda and vinegar, they react together. When the vinegar fizzes, a gas called carbon dioxide is produced. A similar thing happens when a volcano erupts. Hot rock melts and produces gases. Because gases take up more space than solids, pressure builds up, and the gases erupt through the Earth's surface.

How are mountains made?

Mountains are bigger than hills. They reach up much higher than the land around them. Some mountains have steep sides and sharp, jagged peaks, but others have gentler slopes and more rounded peaks. A group of mountains is called a range. The Alps, in Europe, are a well-known mountain range. Many mountains are covered with snow all year-round. It is often very cold and windy on the mountainside, and conditions can be very difficult for the people, animals, and plants trying to live there.

In the mountains

chamois   cattle   waterfall

golden eagle   phlox   skier

▼ **Smooth peaks**
Over a very long time, the rocks are slowly worn away to form more-rounded mountains.

▼ **Highest mountains**
These often have jagged peaks.

▼ **Alpine village**
Tiny villages are dotted across the Alps of Europe. Many of the people who live there are farmers.

word search

mountaineering climbing mountains.
peak the top of a mountain.
range a group of mountains.

Who first climbed to the top of the world's highest mountain?

Mountaineering is a difficult sport, but it is also very popular. Many people have tried to climb the 29,035 feet (8,850 meters) to the top of Mount Everest, the world's highest mountain. The first two people to reach the peak, in 1953, were Edmund Hillary, from New Zealand, and Tenzing Norgay, from Nepal. Mountaineers wear special clothes and boots and carry equipment such as ropes, spikes, clips, and ice axes.

suggest

Suggest why people in the mountains might live differently from those on lower ground.

▼ **How mountains are formed**
Mountains are formed in different ways.

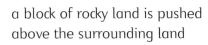
land is squeezed sideways, making wavy folds in the rock

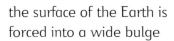
a block of rocky land is pushed above the surrounding land

the surface of the Earth is forced into a wide bulge

Mount Everest is as high as 20 Empire State Buildings.

Water on the move

A river makes a long journey from the mountains to the ocean. Sometimes it joins with another river before reaching the coast. At the beginning, the river is quite shallow and flows quickly through steep mountains and hills. Farther down, where the land is less steep, the river becomes wider as it winds through the valley. Towns and cities are located beside many rivers. People use the river water for drinking and washing, and for their crops. Rivers are also used as a form of transportation.

delta

word search

coast where the sea meets the land.
lake area of water surrounded by land.
transport carry something from one place to another.

▲ Deltas
As the river nears the ocean, some of the soil, rocks, and sand that it is carrying settles to the bottom. Sometimes this dropped material builds up into a piece of land called a delta.

▼ Lakes
A lake is an area of water that is surrounded by land. The world's biggest lake is actually called the Caspian Sea!

this lake formed when water filled a hollow in the rocky land

this lake has formed in the crater of a sleeping volcano

a concrete wall, called a dam, has been built across a river to create this lake

The longest river, the Nile, flows for more than 4,100 miles (6,600 kilometers).

research

What is the name of the river that runs closest to where you live? Can you find out where the river starts and ends?

can you find?

lake   waterfall   valley   river mouth   river   stream   bend

Changing the shape of the land

All around us the land is slowly changing shape. Although rocks are very hard, they can still be worn away into new shapes. Sometimes this wearing-away, which is called erosion, takes millions of years. Wind carries sand and dust that wear away rocks, often into unusual shapes. When water gets into cracks in rocks and then freezes, it splits the rocks open, making small pieces break off. At the coast, waves pound against the cliffs, and over time they are often worn away. Sometimes the ocean wears away a large hole in a cliff to form a cave.

word search

erosion the wearing-away of something.
stalactite a stony spike that hangs down from the roof of a cave.
stalagmite a stony pillar on the floor of a cave.

Erosion

1. underground caves form in the rock
2. rocks are worn away into unusual shapes
3. waves wear away sea cliffs
4. rain freezes in rocks causing small pieces to break off
5. rivers carry small rock pieces, which help to wear away land

cave

column

stalactite

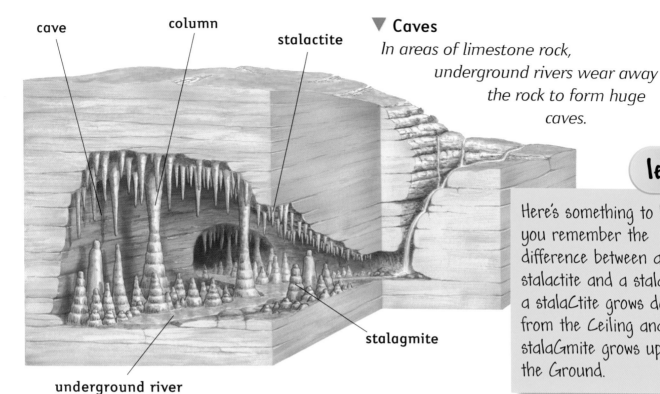

underground river

stalagmite

▼ **Caves**

In areas of limestone rock, underground rivers wear away the rock to form huge caves.

learn

Here's something to help you remember the difference between a stalactite and a stalagmite: a stalaCtite grows down from the Ceiling and a stalaGmite grows up from the Ground.

The rainbow python

The first thing the great god Mawu made when he was creating the world was Dan Ayido Hwedo. Dan Ayido was a python or rainbow snake. The python carried Mawu in his mouth as he traveled around making the world.

At night the python's droppings became mountains. Soon the world was covered with mountains, trees, and animals. Mawu realized it was too heavy and was sinking into the sea. Mawu asked Dan Ayido to save the world by holding it up. The python made his long body into a huge coil so the world could rest on his back. Dan Ayido usually lies still, but sometimes he wriggles and then the Earth shakes.

African myth

What were the mountains made from? What do we call the Earth shaking?

Places without water

Imagine a place where the Sun shines every day and it's baking hot. At night, the skies are clear and it's very cold. Hardly any rain ever falls. This is what conditions are like in a hot desert. Deserts can be cold places, too. In the far north and far south of the world are the ice deserts, where very little rain falls each year. It is difficult for living things to survive in the desert. Animals often have to travel a long way just to find water.

▲ **Desert plants**
The desert is a colorful place after rain because many plants are able to grow flowers.

investigate

How many of the world's deserts can you find in your atlas?

▶ **Icy wasteland**
Penguins are some of the few living things to survive in the polar desert of Antarctica.

▼ **Hot deserts**
Here are some of the plants and animals that live in the Sonoran Desert in the United States.

1. rattlesnake
2. roadrunner
3. kangaroo rat
4. jackrabbit
5. scorpion
6. elf owl
7. coyote
8. cacti

word search

cacti desert plants that store water.

A dry and dusty desert

In a desert the Sun beats down on the dry and dusty land. Only prickly cacti grow. But there are some signs of life. Can you see the snake wriggling in the sand?

You will need

- deep plastic tray · pencil
- dry sand · two small cacti plants
- selection of small rocks and pebbles
- small insects or snakes made from modeling clay

Remember to water the plants once a month.

1 Place a layer of pebbles in the base of the tray. Fill the tray with sand.

Roll out a long snake shape using different colored modeling clay.

2 Plant the cacti and cover their bases with pebbles. Make interesting patterns with the rocks and pebbles and draw snake tracks in the sand with the tip of a pencil. Make a snake from clay and place it under a rock, asleep in the shade!

Find out about dust storms on page 43.

On the grasslands

A large part of the world is covered by open areas of grasslands. These areas have different names across the world. The huge, wide plains in the middle of North America are called prairies. The bare, dry grasslands of central Asia are called steppes. The hot grasslands of East Africa are called savannahs. Natural grasslands are important in providing food for wild animals. Many grassland areas, such as the North American prairies, have become important farming areas. Wheat, corn, and other crops are grown there for food.

▲ **Farming on grasslands**
The prairies of North America are some of the richest farmland in the world.

▼ **Herds of cattle**
Cowboys called gauchos take care of beef cattle on the pampas (grasslands) of Argentina, South America.

word search

pampas grassland in South America.
prairie grassland in North America.
savannah grassland in East Africa.
steppe grassland in central Asia.

There are more than 9,000 different kinds of grass.

research

Look for other books on grasslands. Read about the different kinds of animals that live there.

▲ **Living on grasslands**

These wide, grassy plains are the steppes of central Asia. People called nomads move around the plains, looking for new grass for their animals to eat. They live in round tents called yurts.

The lion loses his lunch

As a hungry lion prowled across the grassy plains, he came across a sleeping rabbit. The lion licked his lips, his mouth watering. "Lunch – how delicious," he thought.

Just as he was about to pounce, he heard rustling and the pounding of hooves. A zebra dashed out of the bushes. The lion hesitated. A zebra would make a much bigger meal. The lion chased after the zebra, but the zebra was too fast. At last the lion gave up, and the zebra was soon far away.

The lion turned around and padded silently back to where the rabbit had been sleeping. She was nowhere to be seen.

Like the zebra, the rabbit had also escaped – and the lion had foolishly lost his lunch.

Aesop fable

What do you think the lion learned? What other grassland animals do lions eat?

In the forest

Forests are large areas of land covered with trees. Tropical rain forests grow in places where it is hot and wet year-round. The largest one is the Amazon rain forest in Brazil. Forests made up of green, leafy trees, such as oak and beech, that lose their leaves in winter and grow new ones in spring are called deciduous forests. Forests that grow in cold places, such as mountains, are usually coniferous forests. Most of the trees in these forests, such as spruce and fir, are evergreen trees, which means they keep their leaves year-round.

▲ **Autumn colors**
The green leaves of the maple tree change to red, orange, and yellow before falling to the ground.

word search

coniferous trees with cones instead of flowers.
deciduous trees that lose their leaves in winter.
evergreen trees that keep their leaves year-round.

trees take in
carbon dioxide

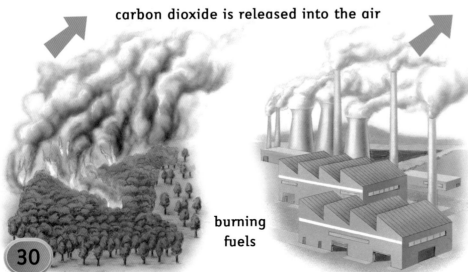

carbon dioxide is released into the air

burning fuels

▶ **Rain forest canopy**
In the rain forest, the tops of the tall trees make a thick roof, or canopy, over the forest floor.

▶ **Needlelike leaves**
The leaves of some evergreen trees are shaped like needles.

▲ **Planting new trees**
New trees are being planted to replace the ones that people have cut down.

▲ **Deforestation**
People cut down forests to get wood for building and paper-making, and to burn as firewood. They also clear the land for crops to grow and animals to graze.

look

Look carefully around you. How many things can you see that are made from trees?

trees give off oxygen

you breathe in air containing oxygen

you breathe out carbon dioxide

trees take in carbon dioxide

◀ **Taking care of our trees**
Trees have a very important job to do. They give off oxygen, a gas we need in the air that we breathe. At the same time, they take in carbon dioxide, a gas given off when we burn fuels such as coal, oil, and gas. Too much carbon dioxide gas is now being released into the air. We need to take care of the world's trees so that they can take in this extra carbon dioxide.

31

What's the weather like?

Will it rain today? Is the sun shining? How windy will it be? The rain, snow, clouds, wind, and sunshine make up our weather, which changes from day to day. The weather is very important to all of us and makes a difference as to which clothes we wear each day. People who try to predict what the weather will be like today and in the future are called weather forecasters.

word search

air pressure the force of the air pushing down on the Earth's surface.
barometer an instrument that measures air pressure.
climate the pattern of weather in a place over a long period of time.

▼ **Our weather**
Weather takes place in the air around us. How many different kinds of weather can you see in this picture?

Does the Sun give us hot water?

Yes, it does. We can use the energy from the Sun to heat water, pump water, heat and cool buildings, and even cook food. When we use the Sun's energy in this way, we call it "solar power." In hot countries, special panels on the roofs of houses trap the Sun's heat and use it to provide hot water. We can also turn the energy from the Sun into electricity. Even satellites in space need the Sun's energy. They are fitted with large solar panels that change sunlight into electricity to make the satellites work.

sing

Do you know any songs or rhymes about the weather?

▲ Different climates

The pattern of weather in a place over a long time is called climate. Different places have different types of climate. Above are two places with different climates: a hot, rainy climate (left) and a hot, dry one (right).

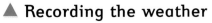

anemometer measures wind speed

weather vane shows the direction of the wind

rain gauge measures the amount of rainfall

thermometer measures temperature

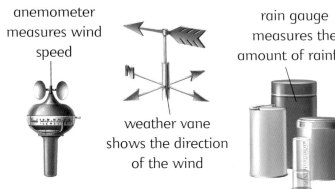

All kinds of weather

snow   sunshine   rain

rainbow   clouds   frost

▲ Recording the weather

Weather stations around the world use different instruments to record weather.

What's the weather like?

Make this weather chart so that your friends will know what to wear each day!

1 Take the sheet of construction paper and ask an adult to help you cut a 3-inch (7½-centimeter) hole in the center. Decorate each corner with a spring, summer, autumn, and winter scene.

2 Ask an adult to help you divide the circle of construction paper into six equal segments. Choose six different types of weather and draw a picture of each within each segment of your circle.

3 Using the paper fastener, attach the circle behind the large sheet of construction paper, making sure that one of the six segments can be clearly seen through the cut-out circle on your sheet of construction paper.

You will need
- large sheet and circle, 10 in (25 cm) diameter, of construction paper
- paper fastener • pencil
- scissors • felt markers

What season is it?

When winter ends each year, the weather becomes warmer and the days are longer. It's spring. Winter and spring are seasons — times of the year when the weather changes and the days become shorter or longer. Some places have four seasons in a year: spring, summer, autumn, and winter. In summer, the weather is warmer and there are more hours of daylight in each day. In winter, it is colder and the days are shorter. In other places, especially those near the Equator, there are only two seasons — a rainy one and a dry one.

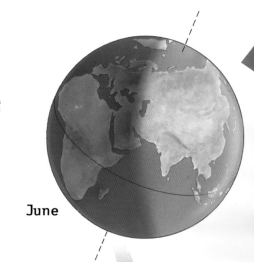

June

Between March and September, the northern half of the world slants toward the Sun. It is summer in this half and winter in the southern half.

◀ **Never-ending days**
In the middle of summer, the Sun never sets in the far north or far south of the world. It is daytime all day long. In north Norway, these places are known as the Lands of the Midnight Sun.

 Who sleeps in the winter?

Many animals, such as bears and squirrels, have a long sleep in winter. This is called hibernation. They find a safe place where they are protected from the cold weather. These animals eat extra food before the winter so that they can survive without food for most of their winter sleep.

▶ **Monsoons**
In parts of India and Asia, very large amounts of rain fall for about three months each year. This rainy time is known as the monsoon season.

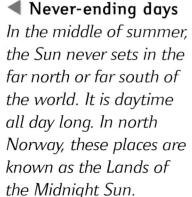

March

Between September and March, the southern half of the world is tilted toward the Sun. It is summer here and winter in the northern half.

Sun

December

Equator

September

think

How many animals can you think of that sleep throughout winter?

▲ **The Earth moves around the Sun**
Seasons happen because the Earth travels around the Sun once each year. As it travels, different parts of the Earth slant toward the Sun.

▼ **Seasons bring about change**
The seasons bring changes in the natural world. Some trees lose their leaves each autumn and grow new ones the following spring.

word search

Equator an imaginary line around the middle of the Earth.
monsoon a strong wind that brings heavy rains.

spring

summer

autumn

winter

Persephone in the Underworld

Spring, summer, autumn, winter – the seasons change **without fail.** The ancient Greeks told a story of how the seasons came to be.

1 When the world was new, it was always summer. The goddess Demeter took care of the Earth. She watered the plants and crops, and picked flowers with her beautiful daughter Persephone.

2 Below the Earth, Pluto was king of the underworld, where it was always dark and gloomy. Sometimes he climbed to the banks of the River Styx to look at the Earth. One day he saw Persephone. He had never seen anyone so beautiful and he fell in love with her instantly. Pluto wanted Persephone to be his wife.

Pluto harnessed his chariot. He snatched Persephone and thundered back to the underworld. "Don't be afraid," he said. "I love you. I will make you my queen."

Who was king of the Greek gods?

3 On Earth, Demeter searched for Persephone and forgot all about her work. When she had almost given up hope she sat by the River Styx. The water whispered what had happened.

Demeter ran to Zeus, the king of the gods, for help.

"If Persephone eats anything in the underworld she must stay," said Zeus. "Let me send Hermes, my messenger, to find out."

4 In the underworld, Persephone ate nothing at all. One day Pluto held out a pomegranate. It smelled delicious, and when twelve seeds were dropped into Persephone's hand, she lifted them to her lips.

5 Just at that moment, Hermes arrived in the underworld. "Stop!" he shouted. But it was too late. Persephone had eaten half the seeds. "Now you must stay here forever," said Hermes.

6 Finally Zeus decided what would happen. "Because Persephone ate six seeds, she will live in the underworld for six months of the year. For the other six months, she will return to her mother."

That is why in spring and summer when Demeter is happy, the sun shines. In autumn, when Persephone goes back to the underworld, flowers die and trees shed their leaves as Demeter cries.

Greek myth

How many pomegranate seeds did Persephone eat?

It's raining!

Water falls from the clouds as rain.
Sometimes it falls to the ground as drizzle or sleet. If the air is really cold, the water inside the clouds freezes. It forms tiny crystals of snow that stick together to become snowflakes. We need rain to fill our rivers and lakes and to give us water to drink. Without rain, the soil would be too dry for plants to grow. Sometimes very heavy rain causes floods. When a place has little or no rain for a long time, we say it has a drought.

thin, wispy clouds appear at the very top of the sky

▶ **Frosty window**
Frost is the sparkly white covering that you can see outside your window on a cold winter morning.

word search

drizzle very light rain with small drops.
droplet a very tiny drop.

water droplets form in clouds

warm air cools

water droplets form raindrops

rain falls to the ground

warm, wet air rises

▶ **How rain and snow fall**
Rain falls when water droplets inside a cloud join together and become too heavy to stay in the cloud. They fall from the clouds as raindrops.

land

ocean

38

low clouds that cover the whole sky like a blanket often bring drizzle and fog

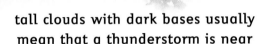

tall clouds with dark bases usually mean that a thunderstorm is near

▲ **Different types of clouds**
Clouds come in many different shapes and sizes.

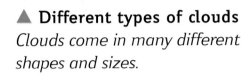

▲ **Hailstones**
A hailstone is a lump of ice. Most hailstones are the same size as peas, but sometimes they are as big as oranges. Hailstones are hard and can damage windows, cars, and plants.

▶ **Snowflakes**
A snowflake is made up of lots of tiny crystals of ice. There are many different shapes of snowflakes, but each one has six sides.

◀ **Rainbows**
You can often see a rainbow in the sky when the Sun shines after a shower of rain. The raindrops break up the rays of sunlight into different colors, forming a multi-colored rainbow.

draw

Draw your own rainbow. Can you name the seven colors of a rainbow?

Mount Wai-'ale-'ale in Hawaii has as many as 350 rainy days a year.

It's stormy!

On a stormy day the sky fills with huge dark clouds. Inside each cloud are millions of droplets of water. Strong winds blow, and it rains heavily. At the same time you might hear a loud crack of thunder, and see bright streaks of lightning flash across the sky. Each flash of lightning is really an enormous spark of electricity. Lightning is so hot that it heats up the air around it. The heated air expands and collides with colder air, causing the crashing sound that we hear as thunder.

▲ **Stormy weather**
Dark storm clouds bring heavy rain as well as thunder and lightning.

word search

collide crash into.
expand become larger.

▲ **God of thunder**
Long ago, the people of northern Europe worshiped a storm god called Thor. They thought he made lightning by throwing a hammer across the sky and that thunder was the noise of his chariot wheels.

3
Gentle breeze: leaves and twigs move, and flags flutter.

7
Nearly gale: trees sway from side to side, and it is hard to walk in the wind.

11
Violent storm: winds are very strong and violent, and cause damage to buildings.

remember

What causes the loud cracks of thunder during a storm? Write down as many words as you can think of that describe what you might see and hear during a thunderstorm.

▲ **Measuring how hard the wind blows**
Weather forecasters use a set of numbers called the Beaufort Scale to measure wind speed. The scale from 0 to 12 describes what happens to outdoor things when the wind speed increases from a soft breeze to a hurricane.

Are thunder and lightning dangerous?

A long time ago, people thought that thunder was the noise made by the gods when they were angry with someone on the Earth. People also believed that lightning was a weapon of the gods. Today, we understand what causes thunder and lightning. When lightning happens very high in the air, it might damage nearby aircraft, but not people or objects on the ground. But when lightning does reach the ground, it can cause fires and damage trees and tall buildings — and it can kill people. The loud noises made by crashing thunder, however, do not harm us.

▼ **Storm damage**
A very powerful storm can blow trees over and pull roofs off houses.

Lightning flash

Thunder and lightning can be very exciting.
Lightning is a giant spark of electricity.

1 Lay the spatula across the top of the drinking glass. Rub the Styrofoam block across the sweater for one minute. Immediately place the block on the spatula.

2 Hold your finger about ½ in (one centimeter) from the handle of the spatula and a spark of electricity will leap across, giving you quite a surprise.

You will need
- Styrofoam block
- woolen sweater
- metal spatula
- drinking glass

Ask a grown-up to help you with this simple, safe experiment.

Find out more about why lightning happens by reading page 40.

Swirling storms

Very violent weather can rip trees out of the ground, hurl cars through the air, and flatten buildings. These storms occur in warm parts of the world. The storms start above the ocean and travel toward land, bringing powerful swirling winds and lashing rain. These storms are called hurricanes. In Asia, they are called cyclones or typhoons. Hurricane winds often cause widespread damage. Weather forecasters use special equipment to follow the path of a hurricane. They give each hurricane a name, and warn people when and where it will arrive.

explore

Look for a weather vane (wind vane) near your home. Can you figure out in which direction the wind is blowing?

storm cloud

▶ **The calm inside a storm**
In the center of a hurricane is a calm area called the "eye." The strong winds around it blow at around 200 miles (320 kilometers) per hour — the same speed as the fastest racing cars.

twisting funnel of storm

word search

funnel a tubelike shape with one wide end.
generate to make or produce.
turbine a device that is turned by wind, water, or steam to provide power.

▶ **Twisting winds**
A tornado is a small but very powerful twisting wind. It sucks up everything in its path like a giant vacuum cleaner. Tornadoes are also called "twisters."

dust, soil, and garbage are sucked up

▲ Dust and sandstorms
These kind of storms often occur in North Africa, where the wind whips up clouds of dust and sand. They usually happen in dry, dusty places, and can take place over great stretches of desert and land.

How does the wind help us?

The wind is not always harmful — it can be helpful, too. For hundreds of years, people have used the power of the wind to turn the sails of their windmills. The windmills were used to grind corn and other types of grain, and later on to pump water. Today, huge wind turbines use wind power to generate electricity. Sometimes lots of turbines are built in one place to create a "wind farm." They generate enough electricity for whole towns and cities.

Odysseus and the storm

Odysseus was a Greek warrior who fought in the great war against Troy. After the war, he sailed for home, but his journey was full of danger and adventure.

Odysseus let his tired crew rest on the island of the Sun god, Hyperion, on the condition they did not touch Hyperion's sacred cattle. But Zeus, the king of the gods, sent a terrible storm. For a whole month, a gale whipped up the waves. It was impossible to fish, and Odysseus and his men began to starve. One day as Odysseus was praying, his men killed and roasted one of the cows.

Hyperion was furious and called to Zeus. When Odysseus' ship set sail, Zeus hit it with a tornado. The ship's mast snapped, and the crew drowned. Only Odysseus, who had not eaten, was saved.

Greek myth

43

Which city did Odysseus fight against? What is the Greek Sun god called?

Amazing wonders of the natural world

Have you ever seen a waterfall shaped like a horseshoe? Or a huge arch made of pinkish-red rocks? Or an iceberg ten times bigger than a house? All these things are part of the world around us — and they were made by natural forces, not by people. Wind and water are two of the forces that help to create natural wonders. The Grand Canyon in the USA was once solid rock. Over many, many years the water of the Colorado River has carved a valley out of the rock. It is over 1 mile (1½ kilometers) deep, almost three times the height of the world's tallest skyscraper. The natural world is filled with some amazing sights.

▶ **Old Faithful**
A geyser in the ground in Yellowstone National Park, USA, blasts hot water high into the air about every 76 minutes.

◀ **Uluru (Ayers Rock)**
A large loaf-shaped rock in central Australia.

look

How many natural wonders do you know about near your home? Find out how they were made.

Namib Desert
The huge sand dunes on this page are in the south-west of Africa.

The largest iceberg ever seen was 210 miles (335 kilometers) long.

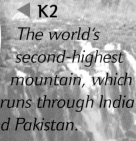

◀ **K2**
The world's second-highest mountain, which runs through India and Pakistan.

◀ **Giant's Causeway**
A collection of around 40,000 rocky pillars on the coast of Northern Ireland.

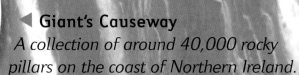

◀ **Grand Canyon**
A deep valley filled with colorful rocks in the USA.

▶ **Rainbow Bridge**
A natural bridge made of rock in Utah, USA.

▼ **Durdle Door**
Waves have created this spectacular sea arch off the coast of Dorset in southern England.

◀ **Cappadocia**
Strange rock formations in Turkey shaped by wind and water.

Victoria Falls
The spectacular waterfall pictured on this page is on Africa's Zambezi River.

The Earth's riches

Every second, people take something from the natural world and use it. We catch fish from the ocean to eat. We cut down trees to get timber for building and making paper, and to burn as firewood. We dig coal out from under the ground and drill oil and gas from deep under the ground and ocean, too. We remove stone from the Earth — this is called quarrying. All these things — fish, timber, coal, oil, stone, and gas — are natural resources. Even the food that farmers grow is a natural resource. We have to be careful not to use up, or deplete, too many resources because some will run out one day.

▼ **What do we take from the Earth?**
Find the Earth's natural resources in this picture:

1 coal mining   5 tin mining
2 farming   6 fishing
3 quarrying stone 7 oil drilling
4 tree felling

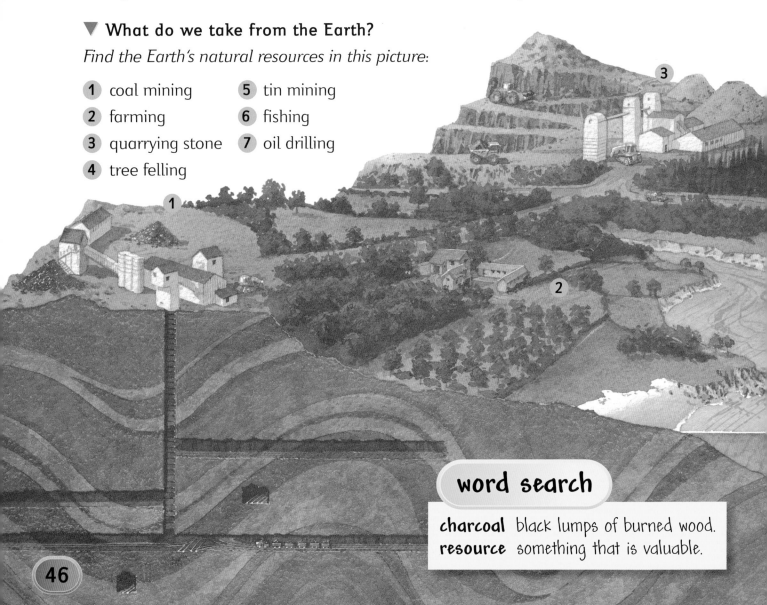

word search

charcoal black lumps of burned wood.
resource something that is valuable.

furniture

paper

rubber

cellophane

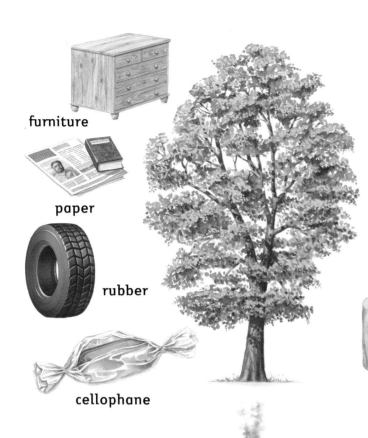

◀ **What do we make from trees?**
Trees are cut down for many reasons. Wood and other parts of certain trees provide us with many different things.

charcoal   cork   nuts

maple syrup

fabric

identify

Look around your home. Make a list of all the things that are made from natural resources.

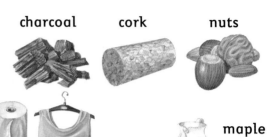

Caring for our world

We are damaging the world around us. Our cars, trucks, factories, and power plants fill the air with dirty gases. We pour harmful chemicals onto soil and into rivers and oceans, and tankers sometimes spill oil into the ocean. We cut down too many trees. We know that we have to take better care of our world. This means releasing fewer harmful wastes into the land, water, and air. We should save more materials by recycling rather than throwing them away. And we have to find new ways of traveling to reduce the waste gases from motor vehicles.

▲ **Cutting down trees**
We are losing too many of the world's trees.

word search

power plant a place that produces large amounts of electricity.
recycle to turn waste into materials that can be used again.

record

Make a list of all the materials that you recycle in your home.

▼ **Oil spills and poisoned waters**
  These kill fish and wildlife.

▲ **Dirty air**
Exhaust fumes cause pollution of our air.

What you can do to help

recycle bottles   recycle newspapers

save water   pick up litter   save energy

▶ Recycling glass

Empty glass bottles and jars are recycled and made into new glass objects.

drinks are sold in glass bottles

recycling bottles

recycled bottles are filled with drinks

the mixture is melted in a huge furnace

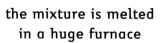

broken glass is mixed with sand and other materials

melted glass is dropped into a bottle mold

What is the ozone layer?

A thin layer of gas called ozone surrounds the Earth. It protects us from the Sun's harmful rays. But we have been destroying this layer by burning fuels such as wood and oil and by releasing chemicals into the air. These chemicals are used to make aerosols work or in refrigerators. The chemicals have made the ozone layer very thin in certain places, for example, over the North Pole and the South Pole. Harmful UV (ultraviolet) rays can pass through these thinner layers and reach us on Earth, where they cause serious sunburn and other damage to people's skin.

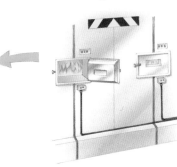

satellite view of Antarctica showing ozone hole (dark blue)

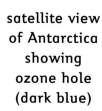

Our planet Earth

High above the Earth, where there is almost no air, is the beginning of space. It stretches out in every direction and goes on forever – no one knows where it ends. Our Earth is just one tiny speck in space. It is one of nine objects called planets that travel around the Sun. The Earth is the only one of these planets where we know definitely that there are living things. It is the only known planet with an atmosphere that contains the right amount of oxygen – the important gas that animals, including human beings, need to stay alive.

▲ **Layers of air**
The layers of air that surround the Earth make up its atmosphere. Beyond this, about 125 miles (200 kilometers) above the Earth's surface, is the beginning of space.

word search

astronaut someone who travels into space.
atmosphere the layers of air that surround the Earth.
planet a large object that travels around the Sun.
space shuttle a spacecraft that visits space over and over again.

describe

Imagine you're an astronaut on board the space shuttle. Describe what Earth looks like from space.

▶ **Different gases**
The air in the Earth's atmosphere contains different gases. The most important are nitrogen and oxygen. Air also contains very tiny amounts of other gases.

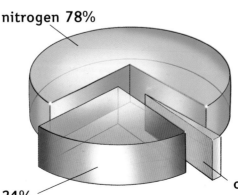

nitrogen 78%

oxygen 21%

other gases 1%

Spacewalking
*This astronaut from the space shuttle
is on a space walk. You can see part
of the Earth behind him.*

The temperature on the surface of the Sun is about 10,000°F (5,500°C).

What is the Sun?

Did you know that the Sun is really a star?

It is one of millions and millions of stars in the sky. Are you wondering why the Sun appears to be bigger and brighter than all the other stars? It is because the Sun is much nearer to the Earth than any other star. The Sun is nearly 93 million miles (150 million kilometers) from the Earth. The next-nearest star is more than 260,000 times farther away from us. Like other stars, the Sun is a huge fiery ball of very hot gases. It is over 109 times wider than the Earth.

energy flows out

core

solar flare

surface

sunspot

design

Design a poster to warn people about the dangers of looking directly at the Sun.

!
DANGER
You must never look directly at the Sun. Its very strong light will damage your eyes.

▲ **Inside the Sun**
Lots of energy is produced in the center of the Sun, the core. This energy flows out to the surface. It then passes into space and travels toward the Earth, mainly as warmth and light.

Who worships the Sun?

Long, long ago, many people believed that the Sun was a god, and they worshiped it. The people of ancient Egypt thought their Sun god sailed in a boat across the sky. In many countries, people made carvings and pictures of their Sun gods. They built special temples and other buildings to honor them. Can you see the Sun god's face in the center of this stone? It was made by the Aztec people of Mexico over 500 years ago.

word search

core the center of something.
solar flare a bright burst of light that shoots out from the Sun.
sunspot a darker, cooler area on the Sun's surface.

▶ **Light traveling in space**

Light from the Sun travels through space to the Earth. It takes 8 minutes and 20 seconds to reach us. Light from the next-nearest star would take 4¼ years to reach the Earth!

Making rainbows

Have you ever seen a rainbow and wondered how it happens? Find out in this experiment.

1 Mark out a rectangle ½ inch (1 centimeter) wide and 1½ inches (4 centimeters) long in the center of the cardboard. Cut this out. Use tape to attach the cardboard upright to the side of the glass.

2 Place the sheet of white paper on a sunny windowsill. Position the glass on the paper so that sunlight shines through the hole in the cardboard and water and onto the paper. As the light shines through the water, it will break up into red, orange, yellow, green, blue, indigo, and violet and shine a rainbow onto the paper.

You will need

- postcard-size piece of white cardboard · tape
- scissors · ruler
- drinking glass full to the brim with water · pencil
- sheet of white paper

This experiment works best in the early morning or late afternoon. If it is cloudy, use a strong flashlight instead of sunlight.

Find out more about rainbows on page 39.

The Sun's family

Our planet Earth is part of a family of planets. All these planets move around the Sun. Some, such as Earth and Mars, have their own moons. These moons travel around the planets. In the spaces between the planets there are other bits and pieces. These are smaller pieces of rock called asteroids, lumps of rock and ice called comets, and lots of other tiny specks of dust and gas. Together, all these things in space make up the Sun's family, which we call the Solar System.

word search

asteroid a chunk of rock in space.
meteoroid a piece of dust or rock in space.
solar to do with the Sun.

▶ **The Solar System**
The Solar System is made up of the Sun, eight planets, and all the other objects traveling around the Sun.

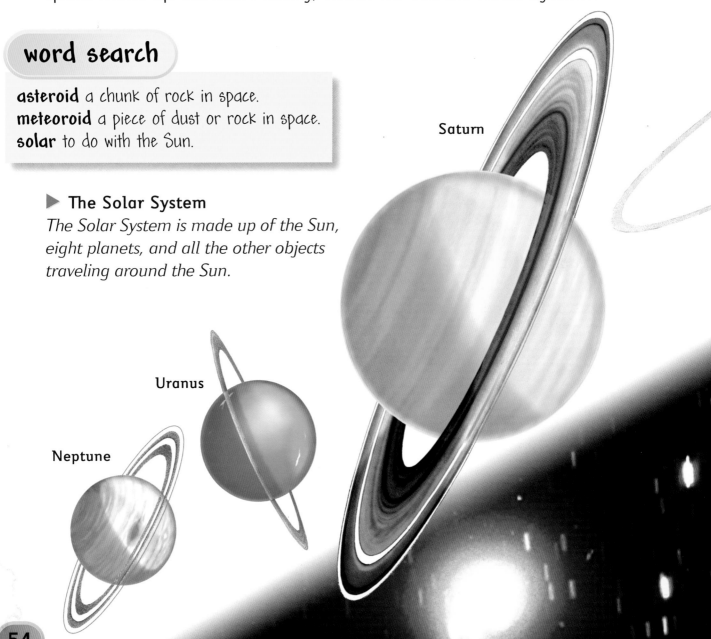

Saturn

Uranus

Neptune

Why is the Sun's family called the Solar System?

Sun

Mercury

Venus

Earth

Mars

Jupiter

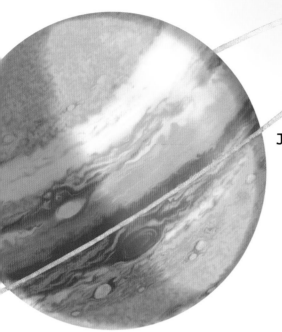

▲ **Taking pictures**

This spacecraft called Galileo was sent into space to take pictures of planets.

▼ **Objects in space**

As well as the planets, smaller objects in space are moving around the Sun.

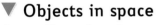

comet

asteroid

meteoroid

◄ **Comets**

Sometimes a bright comet appears in the sky above Earth. This one, called Hale-Bopp, was seen in the night sky in 1997.

A line of 109 Earths could be placed across the Sun's width.

Around the Sun

The four planets closest to the Sun – Mercury, Venus, Earth, and Mars – are called rocky planets. They are balls of rock. The planets that are farther from the Sun are much bigger. They are enormous balls of gas and liquid. We sometimes call them gas giants. All the planets move in the same direction around the Sun. They travel along oval-shaped paths called orbits.

1 Mercury (88 days)
2 Venus (224.7 days)
3 Earth (365.25 days)
4 Mars (687 days)
5

6 Jupiter (11.9 years)
7 Saturn (29.5 years)
8 Uranus (84 years)
9 Neptune (164.8 years)

▼ **Orbiting planets**
The planets take different amounts of time to orbit the Sun. This is shown on the left in Earth time.

word search

an orbit the path that a planet travels along.
to orbit to travel around something in space.
oval egg-shaped.

◀ **The asteroid belt**

Thousands of asteroids lie in space between the planets Mars and Jupiter. This part of space is called the asteroid belt.

Jupiter

◀ **Rocky and gas planets**

A rocky planet, such as Venus, is made of rock and metal. A gas planet, such as Jupiter, is made up mainly of gas and liquid.

Venus

Sun, planets, and moons

Make this spectacular mobile of our Solar System to hang in your bedroom. The planets are suspended from a large oval of cardboard that has been painted midnight blue and decorated with gold or silver stars.

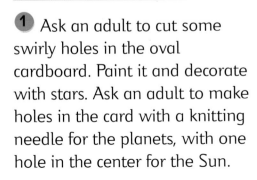

You will need

- oval-shaped cardboard 18 x 14 in (45 x 35 cm)
- tape · glue · paints and paintbrushes · glitter
- thumb tacks · 9 Styrofoam balls in a variety of sizes
- gold thread · star stickers
- knitting needle · cardboard for Saturn's ring

Look at page 56 to find out what colors to paint the planets.

1 Ask an adult to cut some swirly holes in the oval cardboard. Paint it and decorate with stars. Ask an adult to make holes in the card with a knitting needle for the planets, with one hole in the center for the Sun.

2 Paint the Styrofoam balls to look like the planets and the Sun. Cut out a cardboard ring and decorate with glitter. Glue this around Saturn. Carefully push thumb tacks into the planets to make moons. Paint the pinheads yellow. Glue a piece of thread to each Styrofoam ball. Push the other end through a hole in the oval. Hold in place with tape. Hang your mobile from the ceiling.

Find out more about planets on pages 50, 54, 55 and 56.

The Earth and the Moon

The Earth has a hard outside crust made of solid rock. Underneath this crust are layers of liquid rock called the mantle. Deeper down, the core at the center of the Earth is partly solid metal and partly liquid metal. The Earth's neighbor in space is the Moon. It is a natural satellite of the Earth and is about one-quarter of its size. The Moon is rocky too, with highlands, wide flat areas called plains, and large craters. Some people think that these dark and light areas look like a face on the surface of the Moon.

◀ **The Moon traveling around Earth**
The Moon orbits the Earth. It takes 27⅓ days to travel all the way around.

▲ **The Moon**
Can you see the dark-colored plains and the light-colored highland areas in this photo of the Moon?

On the Moon the sky is always black, even in the daytime.

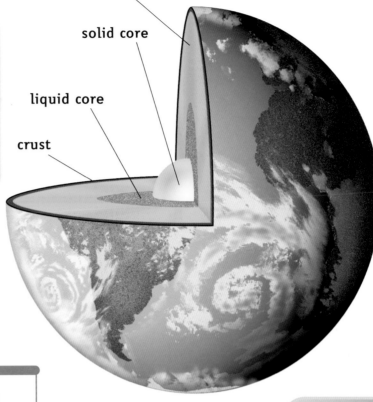

mantle

solid core

liquid core

crust

word search

crater a round hollow in the surface of a planet or a moon.
crust the hard outside of a planet or a moon.
tide the change in sea level caused by the Moon's pull.

▶ **Inside our Earth**

The Earth is a ball of rock. Under the crust are layers of rock and metal called the mantle. At the center of the Earth are two metal layers called the core.

Why does the tide rise and fall each day?

The answer is the Moon! The regular rise and fall of the ocean, called tides, is mostly caused by the Moon's pull on the Earth. The waters directly below the Moon, and on the opposite side of the Earth, receive the strongest pull and so they bulge outward – this is when high tide takes place. At the same time, places in between have low tide. As the Earth spins slowly around, places move in and out of the bulging areas and so the tides rise and fall. In most places there are two high tides and two low tides every 24 hours and 50 minutes.

talk about

What do you see when you look at the Moon? Can you see the face of the 'man in the Moon'?

▼ **Man on the Moon**

In 1969 a human being stepped onto the surface of the Moon for the very first time.

Does the Moon change shape?

When you look into the sky at night, the Moon does not always appear big and round. Sometimes you see half the Moon or just a very thin slice of it. Sometimes you can't see the Moon at all. The Moon reflects light from the Sun. It has no light of its own. As the Moon orbits the Earth, you see different parts of its sunlit side. When you see a Full Moon, the whole sunlit side faces the Earth. When there is a New Moon, the dark side faces the Earth.

▲ **Crescent Moon**
Sometimes you only see a thin bright slice of the Moon in the sky. This is called a Crescent Moon.

identify

Look at the Moon before you go to sleep tonight. Can you match its shape with one of the pictures on this page?

word search

crescent a thin curved shape.
phase a step or stage.
reflect to send back light from a shiny object.

▶ **Light from the Sun**
Like the Earth, half of the Moon is lit up by the Sun's light. The other half is in shadow.

light from Sun

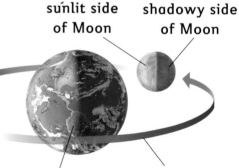

sunlit side of Moon

shadowy side of Moon

Moon's orbit

Earth

▼ **The changing Moon**
The Moon seems to be changing all the time. These changing shapes and sizes are called phases of the Moon. It takes 29½ days to change from a New Moon to a Full Moon and back again.

New Moon	Crescent Moon	First Quarter	Gibbous Moon	Full Moon	Gibbous Moon	Last Quarter	Crescent Moon

Tiny colored balls of glass have been found in soil on the Moon.

Lone Bird and the Moon

Many Native American myths are about nature. The story of Lone Bird tells how the Moon got its face. Long ago, the Chippewa tribe lived on the shores of Lake Superior. Lone Bird was the daughter of Dawn of Day and She Eagle. Many young braves wanted to marry Lone Bird, and Dawn of Day decided they should all run a race. The winner would marry his daughter. Two braves ran faster than any others. Both had loved Lone Bird for a long time. Again and again they raced, determined to make Lone Bird their bride, but they always finished side by side. However many times they raced there was never a winner.

Lone Bird was delighted. She did not want to marry anyone. Summer passed, autumn leaves fell, winter snows covered the lake, then trees blossomed once more. It was spring, yet Lone Bird felt sad. She wondered what would happen to her.

Lone Bird sat on a hill overlooking the lake. The Full Moon rose slowly in the sky. Its round reflection gleamed in the lake. Silver moonlight shone on the hillside and over Lone Bird. She gazed at the Moon. Nothing else seemed as beautiful. She stretched her arms towards the glowing Moon. "I would not feel lonely if I had you to love," she whispered.

The Good Spirit heard Lone Bird and lifted her up to the Moon. When Dawn of Day returned home at night, he looked for his daughter but she was nowhere to be found. Dawn of Day and She Eagle hurried to the hill where Lone Bird often sat. They called to the Good Spirit and looked up to the dark sky and silver Moon. At first they could not believe their eyes. But they clearly saw their daughter, Lone Bird, smiling down at them. If you look up at the next Full Moon, you can see her face for yourself.

Native American myth

The rocky planets

The rocky planets are Mercury, Venus, Earth, and Mars. Mercury is a very hot place because it is closest to the Sun. The heat on Mercury during the day is so great that it could melt tin. Venus passes nearer to the Earth than any other planet. Thick clouds around it reflect the Sun's light, making Venus one of the brightest objects seen from Earth. We often call Mars the red planet. It looks red in the sky because the surface is covered with reddish-brown rocks and soil.

▲ **Poisonous gases**
Venus is surrounded by a thick blanket of gases, which are poisonous. These yellowish-white clouds of gas trap the Sun's heat, making the planet a very hot place.

word search

explore to look around somewhere for the first time.

▼ **Landing on Mars**
In 1997, this vehicle, called Sojourner, *explored Mars. It examined the rocks and soil on its dusty surface.* Sojourner *was carried to Mars by a spacecraft called* Pathfinder *(see page 76).*

▶ Mercury's craters

The surface of Mercury is a bit like the Moon — it is covered with rocky craters. These were probably made when large rocks crashed into the planet.

▲ Volcanoes on Mars

There are volcanoes on the surface of Mars. This one, called Olympus Mons, is the largest. It is three times higher than Mount Everest, the tallest mountain on Earth.

▼ Can you see Venus?

Venus can be seen in the skies just before sunrise or just after sunset. This is why we often call it the morning star or the evening star.

explain

Why is Venus sometimes called the morning star?

Mars has two small moons that look a little bit like giant potatoes.

Giant balls of gas

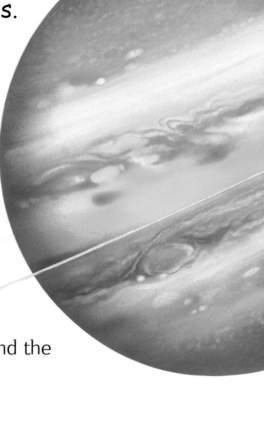

Jupiter and Saturn are the largest of the four planets we call gas giants. Jupiter is so huge that it could swallow 1,000 Earths. It spins around faster than any other planet in the Solar System. Among the clouds wrapped around Jupiter is an enormous storm called the Great Red Spot. This spot is bigger than the Earth. Saturn, the second largest planet, is surrounded by thousands of shining rings. They are really lots of tiny pieces of ice and dust that whiz around the planet but never actually touch it.

word search

astronomer someone who studies space, the stars, and planets.
helium an invisible and very light gas.
hydrogen an invisible gas found in the Sun and other stars.

▼ **Saturn's rings**
The bright rings around Saturn make it one of the most beautiful objects in our Solar System.

◀ **The Great Red Spot**
You can see Jupiter's Great Red Spot through a small telescope. It is wider than the width of the Earth.

Jupiter's Great Red Spot storm has been blowing for more than 300 years!

▼ **Biggest planets in the Solar System**

Jupiter and Saturn are the two biggest planets in the Solar System. They are made up mostly of a mixture of hydrogen and helium gases.

think

Why do you think Jupiter is known as a "gas giant"?

Jupiter and Aeneas

The myths of ancient Rome told of gods and goddesses playing important parts in people's lives. The king of the Roman gods was Jupiter.

After the home of Prince Aeneas of Troy was destroyed in the war with Greece, the Prince escaped and sailed away. He was protected by the goddess Venus, his mother. But the goddess Juno, Jupiter's wife, tried to stop him. She had supported the Greeks during the war. When Aeneas had almost reached safety in Italy, Juno asked the wind god Aeolus to send winds to sink the Trojan ships. But Neptune, god of the seas, calmed the waves and sent the winds back to Aeolus.

Jupiter wanted to be fair. He saw how sad Venus was because Aeneas was in danger. From his palace above the world, Jupiter looked down at the Trojan ships. He promised Aeneas that he and his men would land safely in Italy.

Roman myth

From which city did Aeneas come? Which god of the sea helped the Trojans?

Faraway planets

Uranus and Neptune are faraway planets made of gas and ice. You need a telescope or powerful binoculars to see them from the Earth. Uranus was discovered accidentally, in 1781, by a German astronomer named William Herschel.

At the time, he was studying the stars through a homemade telescope. Together with his sister, Caroline, he continued to study the planets, and noted two moons around Uranus, along with two previously unknown moons of Saturn.

How were planets discovered?

Uranus was the first planet to be discovered with the help of a telescope. William Herschel made this exciting discovery in 1781 using a telescope in his back garden in Bath, England. Astronomers were studying the night skies long before he made his discovery. Over 2,000 years ago, people were making charts of the night sky. Today's astronomers use very powerful telescopes to study the stars and planets.

▲ **Observing Saturn**
Almost 400 years ago, an Italian named Galileo Galilei made his own telescope and looked at the planet Saturn.

word search

crag a steep rock or cliff.
Solar System the Sun and the family of planets, moons, and other objects that move around it.

▼ **Gas and ice planets**
There is a faint system of rings around both Uranus and Neptune. Uranus (shown left) is the only planet in the Solar System that is tipped onto its side.

▼ **The moons of Uranus**
Miranda is one of 15 moons moving around Uranus. It has a surface dotted with valleys and crags.

research

Find out more about telescopes and how they help you see farther.

Bits and pieces in space

Comets are like dirty snowballs in space.
They are lumps of frozen gases, ice, and dust moving around the Sun. When a comet comes near the Sun, the ice melts and some of it turns into gas. Then we see the comet with its bright head and long shining tail. Asteroids are chunks of rock in space — some large asteroids are called minor planets. Some measure 620 miles (1,000 kilometers) across; others are tiny, as small as your fist. Meteoroids are lumps of dust, rock, or metal. Sometimes they fall toward the Earth and produce streaks of light called shooting stars or meteors.

head

▼ **Meteor crater**
Some meteoroids fall through space and crash onto the Earth's surface as meteorites, making a large crater in the ground. The Arizona Meteor Crater in the USA is over 1/2 mile (1 kilometer) wide.

word search

comet a lump of frozen gases, ice, and dust.
shooting star another word for meteor.

comets, meteoroids, and asteroids

Halley's Comet

Can you see the comet at the top of this picture? It's Halley's Comet, which visits our skies every 76 years. This tapestry was made over 900 years ago to tell the story of the Battle of Hastings, which took place in England in 1066. Halley's Comet appeared in the same year.

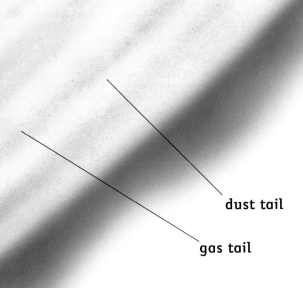

dust tail

gas tail

◄ Comets

A comet's head is a mixture of rock, dust, and ice surrounded by a cloud of gas. Its tail can extend over great distances.

▲ Shooting stars

Meteoroids catch fire as they fall toward Earth. They produce streaks of light called meteors or shooting stars.

retell

Describe what's happening in the scene above from the Bayeux Tapestry. The writing at the top is in Latin. It says: "They admire the star."

American Carolyn Shoemaker has discovered 32 comets – more than anyone else.

Three, two, one . . . lift-off!

On October 4, 1957, the world's first spacecraft, called *Sputnik 1*, blasted off from the Earth. Four years later, a Russian named Yuri Gagarin became the first person to travel into space. His flight lasted 108 minutes. We have learned a lot about the unknown world of space since those early days. Unmanned spacecraft have now visited every planet in the Solar System. People can stay in space for longer and longer, carrying out important scientific work. One Russian cosmonaut spent 438 days on board the Russian space station *Mir*.

▼ **Blasting into space**
Three, two, one . . . lift-off. The space shuttle rocket blasts off into space.

word search

cosmonaut Russian word for "astronaut."

▶ The first spacecraft

The world's first spacecraft, Sputnik 1, circled the Earth in 1957.

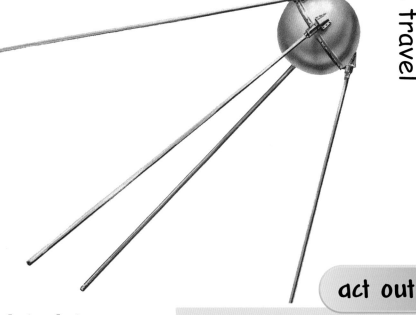

▲ First man in space

Yuri Gagarin was the first human being to travel in space. He circled the Earth in a spacecraft called Vostok 1.

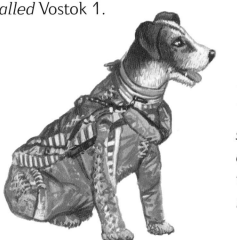

◀ Animals in space

The first living being in space was a Russian dog called Laika. She was sent on a journey into space in 1957.

act out

Imagine you are the Russian cosmonaut Yuri Gagarin about to make the first space flight. Act out the arrival at the spacecraft, strapping yourself into your seat, and getting ready for lift-off.

What do you know about space?

1957	First living being in orbit	Russian	a dog called Laika
1961	First man in space	Russian	Yuri Gagarin
1963	First woman in space	Russian	Valentina Tereshkova
1965	First person to walk in space	Russian	Alexei Leonov
1969	First man on the Moon	American	Neil Armstrong
1971	First space station launched	Russian	*Salyut 1*
1981	First space shuttle flight	American	lasted 54 hours
1994– 1995	Longest human stay in space	Russian	438 days

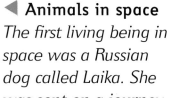

Sputnik 1 was a small metal ball with a radio transmitter and batteries inside it.

Traveling into space

satellite being launched

Most spacecraft cannot reach space on their own – they need the help of powerful rockets to lift off the ground. Space rockets burn huge amounts of fuel. This burning produces hot gases that stream out of the bottom of the rocket, pushing it upward. One of the most powerful rockets was *Saturn V*, which launched spacecraft to the Moon. Early rockets could only be used once, but the booster rockets that launch the space shuttle can be used over and over again.

▶ **The space shuttle**
The space shuttle is the world's first reusable spacecraft. It can carry up to eight people and lots of equipment. It often launches satellites into space.

living quarters

cargo bay

flight deck

◀ **Launching the space shuttle**
This picture shows the launch of the space shuttle with its three main parts (see next page).

word search
cargo things carried inside a vehicle such as a truck or a spacecraft.
launch send a spacecraft into the air.
nozzle a short tube or funnel.
orbiter the main part of the space shuttle that carries the astronauts.

robot arm

▼ Landing the space shuttle
The space shuttle lands back on the Earth like a plane. The parachute helps to slow it down.

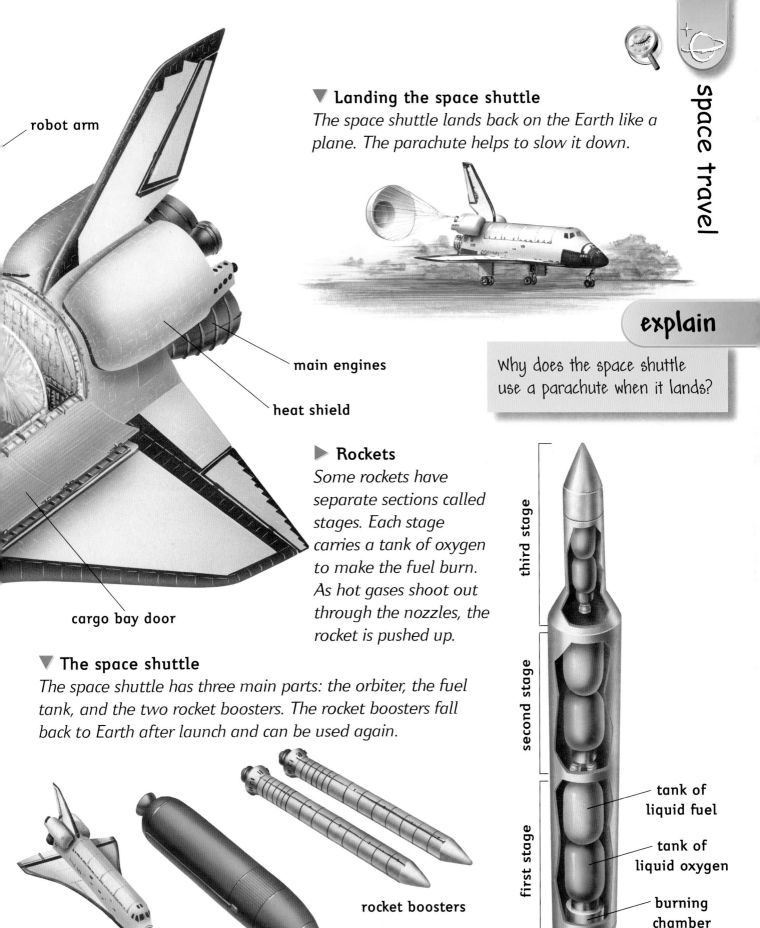

main engines

heat shield

Why does the space shuttle use a parachute when it lands?

▶ Rockets
Some rockets have separate sections called stages. Each stage carries a tank of oxygen to make the fuel burn. As hot gases shoot out through the nozzles, the rocket is pushed up.

cargo bay door

▼ The space shuttle
The space shuttle has three main parts: the orbiter, the fuel tank, and the two rocket boosters. The rocket boosters fall back to Earth after launch and can be used again.

orbiter

fuel tank

rocket boosters

third stage

second stage

first stage

tank of liquid fuel

tank of liquid oxygen

burning chamber

nozzle

stream of hot gases

73

Journey to the Moon

When astronauts landed on the Moon in 1969, it was the first time that anyone had set foot in another part of space. To reach the Moon, they had to leave their *Apollo* spacecraft and travel in the smaller lunar module. Once the module landed on the Moon, they could get out and walk around. Later, astronauts drove across the Moon in a moon buggy. They collected rocks and soil to bring back to Earth. They left behind equipment for scientific experiments — as well as their walking boots and backpacks!

word search

lunar anything to do with the Moon.
module part of a spacecraft.

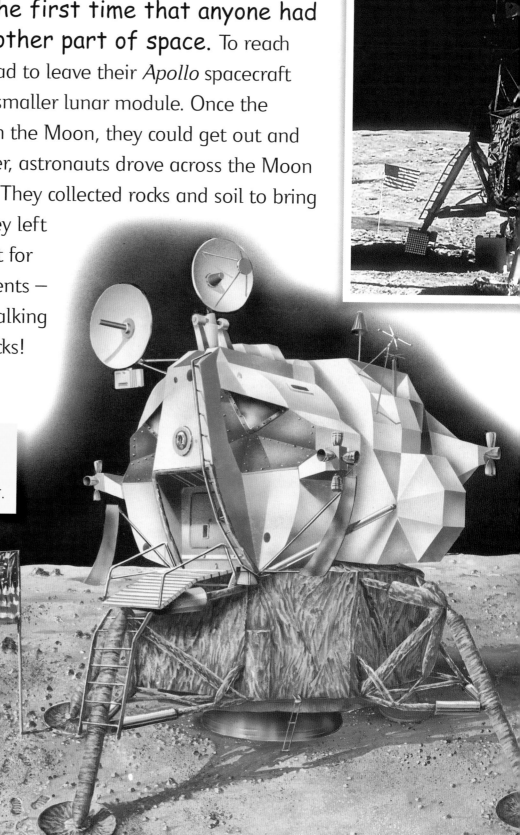

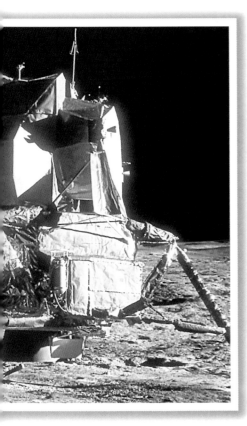

▶ The Moon buggy

Astronauts drove more than 15 miles (25 kilometers) across the Moon in this Moon buggy. The proper name for the vehicle is lunar rover.

◀ Lunar module

High above the Moon, the lunar module separated from the main spacecraft. It fired its engines and then traveled down and landed on the Moon's surface.

tell

Do you know any rhymes or poems about the Moon?

▼ Landings on the Moon

The Apollo 11 lunar module was called Eagle. It landed on the Moon on July 20, 1969. Astronauts from Apollo spacecraft landed on the Moon six times.

Space travel

space walk

Moon crater

Earth from space

lift-off

splash down

What's in space?

By now, all of the planets have been visited by spacecraft.
Unmanned spacecraft take photos and make maps as they fly past the planets. Sometimes they drop small scientific instruments onto the planet's surface. The instruments send information back to the Earth. The spacecraft then fly deeper into space, heading toward the stars. Satellites in space orbiting the Earth send television pictures, telephone calls, and internet messages around the world. Some take photos of the Earth and provide information to help weather forecasters tell us about the weather.

1 parachute is cut
2 balloons inflate
3 *Pathfinder* lands on Mars

▼ **Landing on Mars**
This spacecraft, called Pathfinder, *landed on Mars in 1997. Inside the spacecraft was a small robot vehicle, about the size of a microwave oven, that drove over the planet's surface.*

Pathfinder

robot vehicle

find out

How do television pictures travel from one side of the world to the other? Find out on these pages.

◄ Satellites for communication
This satellite sends television pictures around the world at top speed. It lets you watch an event at the same time it is taking place in a faraway country.

▼ How does a television satellite work?
A satellite in space receives pictures from a television station in one place on the Earth. It beams them to a station in another place.

satellite

▲ Working in space
Astronauts from the space shuttle are working in space.

pictures are
sent as signals

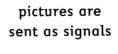
television station

► Satellite picture of Earth
This photo was taken by a satellite in space. It does not show colors as they really are.

77

Satellites help people find out where they are – to the nearest 30 feet (10 meters).

Inside a space station

Imagine tying your sleeping bag to a wall to keep yourself from floating around while asleep! Or brushing your teeth upside down! That's what life is like inside a space station. Astronauts, scientists, and others can live and work in space for months at a time in a space station. The station provides them with the food, water, and oxygen they need to breathe. Spacecraft visit regularly to bring fresh supplies. In the weightless conditions of space, scientists can make some medicines and chemicals more easily than on the Earth. They also find out more about how plants and animals grow.

describe

What would you enjoy most if you had to spend one month inside a space station? And what would you miss?

can you find?

solar panel   *telescope*   *sleeping bags*

▼ International space station

Several countries are involved in building a new space station. It is being assembled bit by bit in space. It is called the International Space Station.

word search

assemble to put together.

▼ Life in space

It can be quite difficult to eat in space!

computer 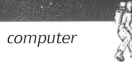 *spacesuit* 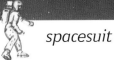 *visiting spacecraft*

Silver spacecraft

This amazing spacecraft contains everything you need to travel around the Universe. You can make and add as many things as you like – comfortable beds, computers, a shower and toilet, fuel burners, and even a miniature robot to do your work!

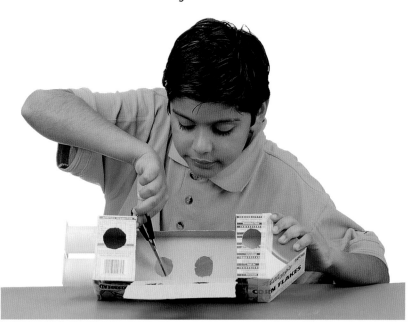

You will need
- a large rectangular and a small cardboard box
- ruler • pencil • paintbrush
- scissors • plastic straws
- paper • cereal boxes
- silver and colored paints
- lots of small boxes, lids, and clean, empty food containers • tape
- small pieces of fabric
- felt markers
- red and yellow tissue paper • small yogurt containers • film cans

1 Cut a corner of the small box to fit the end of the rectangular box. Attach it with tape to make the pointed front of your spacecraft. Cut out circular windows and a door.

Stick red and yellow tissue paper to the back to blast your spaceship into space!

2 Use two yogurt containers to make the fuel burners at the back of the spacecraft. Attach them with tape. Paint the inside and outside of the spacecraft silver. Leave it until the paint is dry.

4 Make some seats from the empty yogurt containers. The instrument panel is made from a small, empty box, painted and decorated with felt-tip pens.

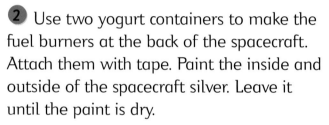

Space travelers need bunk beds to sleep on. Make them from small, empty boxes. Make sleeping bags from fabric cut into rectangles to fit the beds. Make lockers for food from small boxes. You could use plastic camera film cans to make some water bottles.

3 Make a shower from a small, plastic box and a toilet from a small empty food container. Decorate with silver paint.

5 Make a robot to help with the work. Use a small yogurt container and a plastic lid glued to the top. Make holes in the side of the container and insert plastic straws for arms. Paint and decorate your robot.

Before you do this project, save some empty boxes and other containers to make your spacecraft.

Find out more about spacecraft on pages 70, 71, 72, 73, 78 and 79.

Is anyone there?

Do you believe there are other living beings in space?
Do you think they look like us? The Earth is the only planet where we know there is life, but people are always looking for signs of life elsewhere in space. Scientists use very powerful instruments to listen for signals from other parts of space. The *Pioneer* spacecraft that visited Jupiter and Saturn carried special pictures on board. They showed a man, a woman, and the Earth's position in the Solar System – just in case the spacecraft met someone else on the journey.

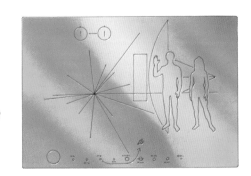

review

Why did the *Pioneer* spacecraft carry pictures of a man and a woman into space?

◀ **Signals from space**
Huge radio telescopes like this one are constantly searching for signals coming from outer space.

▶ **Pictures from Earth**
This is the plate carried by the Pioneer 10 *and* 11 *spacecraft.* Pioneer 10 *was the first spacecraft to reach Jupiter.*

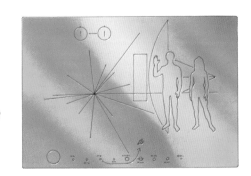

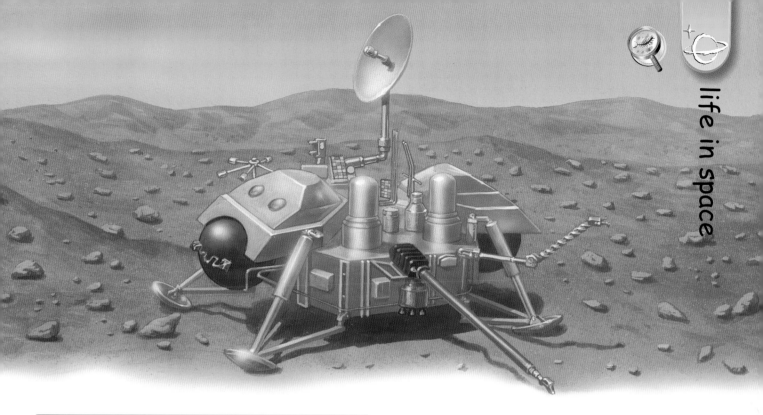

Could we live on another planet?

We can live on the Earth because we have the right amount of warmth from the Sun. We also have plenty of water and oxygen, which is the gas that we need to stay alive. But what would life be like on another planet? Neptune is so far away from the Sun that it would be a very very cold place. We could not survive on Venus because it would be very very hot, and rain filled with acid would pour down from the clouds above. Mercury is so close to the Sun that it would be far too hot during the day and freezing cold at night. Life on Jupiter would also be difficult with high-speed winds and raging storms.

▲ Looking for signs of life

This Viking lander took thousands of photographs of Mars and tested the soil. It did not find any signs of life on the planet.

▶ Flying saucers

Some people claim that this is a "flying saucer" spacecraft from another planet. We call it a UFO, which stands for Unidentified Flying Object. But do you think it's really a spacecraft?

word search

radio telescope *a telescope that can pick up signals from outer space.*

Between 1948 and 1969, sightings of over 12,000 UFOs were reported in the USA.

Watching the stars

▲ **Observatories**
Astronomers use very powerful telescopes to watch the night sky. Telescopes are often placed inside special buildings called observatories.

For thousands of years people have watched the stars twinkling in the night sky. Each night the sky looks a little different — the Moon changes shape and new patterns of stars appear. There are special patterns of bright stars called constellations in the night sky. They were first noticed long ago, and people named them after the shapes they saw. Some were named after animals or people from the stories of ancient Greece, such as Leo, the Lion or Orion, the Hunter. Some have modern names, such as Horologium, the Clock.

look

Which star patterns can you see in the sky tonight?

star patterns in the Northern Hemisphere

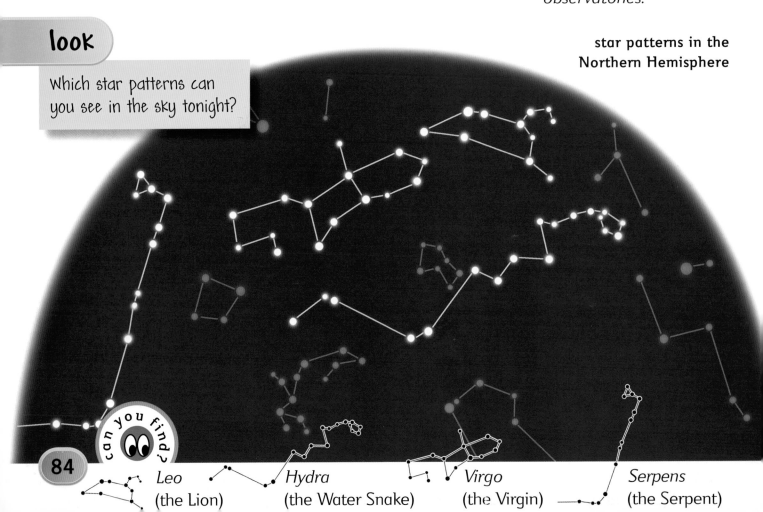

can you find?

84

Leo
(the Lion)

Hydra
(the Water Snake)

Virgo
(the Virgin)

Serpens
(the Serpent)

▼ Watching the stars

You can watch the stars at night with a simple telescope or a pair of binoculars – or just with your own eyes!

word search

constellation a pattern of stars or the name of an area in the night sky.
hemispheres the two halves of the Earth divided into North and South.
observatories buildings that have telescopes for watching the night sky.

▶ Hubble Space Telescope

This huge telescope orbits the Earth. It takes pictures of the stars in space.

star patterns in the
Southern Hemisphere

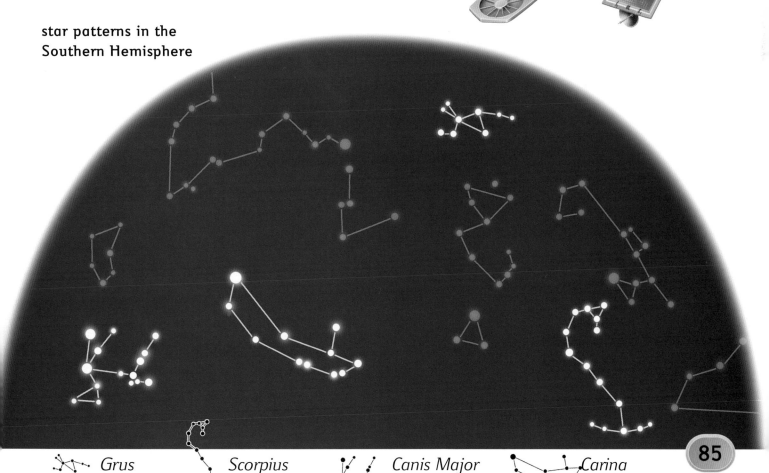

Grus
(the Crane)

Scorpius
(the Scorpion)

Canis Major
(the Great Dog)

Carina
(the Ship's Keel)

85

Millions and millions of stars

Our nearest star is the Sun. Like other stars it is a ball of very hot gases. The Sun appears big and bright in the sky because it is much closer than the other stars. They are far, far away from the Earth. Millions and millions of stars form huge star families called galaxies. The Earth and the Sun are inside a galaxy called the Milky Way, which contains about 100,000 million stars! And the Milky Way is just one of millions and millions of other galaxies in space.

▲ **Taking pictures in space**
This beautiful picture shows a cloud of gas and dust.

▼ **Life of a star**
A star like the Sun starts its life inside a huge cloud of gas and dust. As part of the cloud begins to shrink, the star grows hotter and hotter until it starts to shine brightly. Afterward, the star will grow bigger and bigger and become a red giant star.

red giant

star begins to swell

new star begins to shine

part of the cloud grows smaller and hotter

cloud of dust and gas

word search

galaxy a huge family of stars.
shrink become smaller.
swell become bigger.

A red giant star is about 100 times bigger than our Sun.

▲ Star clusters

This group of stars is the Pleiades. The popular name for it is the Seven Sisters. Can you count the seven brightest stars?

▶ Galaxies

Galaxies come in many different shapes and sizes. This one has a circular shape, with curved arms reaching out from the center – it is a spiral galaxy.

◀ Exploding star

Every star eventually runs out of energy and dies. Big stars die in a huge explosion like the one seen here.

tell

What do we call a family of millions and millions of stars?

Stellar constellation

Lie in bed at night and look at the stars.

Make your own glow-in-the-dark stars from self-hardening clay.

You will need
- glow-in-the-dark self-hardening clay • star-shaped cookie cutter
- rolling pin • double-sided tape
- cookie sheet

1 Roll the clay out on a clean surface. Using a star-shaped cookie cutter, cut out small stars.

2 Harden them according to the manufacturer's instructions, then ask an adult to attach them to your ceiling or wall with double-sided tape.

Always wash your hands after using self-hardening clay.

Deep into space

The Universe is everything that we know about on the Earth, in the Solar System, in the whole of space, and even beyond that. No one knows how big the Universe really is because we cannot see all of it. So no one knows where it ends. We do know that light, the fastest-moving thing, takes billions of years to reach the Earth from faraway parts of the Universe. The Earth is just one very tiny speck in the vast Universe, which contains millions and millions of galaxies.

word search

nebula a cloud of dust and gas in space.
vast very big.

▼ **Clouds of gas and dust**
Clouds of gas and dust are found in space. Sometimes they surround the stars, and sometimes they are in the gaps between stars. This one is called the Horsehead Nebula. How do you think it got its name?

◀ **Watching the night sky**
This is a picture of the Andromeda Galaxy. You can usually see it without a telescope. It looks like a hazy patch in the night sky of the Northern Hemisphere.

draw

Make your own expanding model Universe. Draw lots of galaxies on a blue balloon with a felt marker, then ask an adult to blow it up.

▼ **Deep in space**
The Hubble Space Telescope can look deeper and deeper into space. Its pictures are better than any we have seen before.

You can spot around 2,500 stars when the night sky is clear and dark.

Can you remember?

Now that you have finished reading about the Earth and space, try answering the following questions. Each picture contains a clue — the page number where you will find the answer.

▼ **1** Can you name the ten different features on the area of land shown here?

10

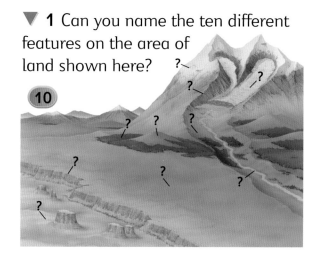

◀ **2** Each of the colored areas on this map is a continent. Can you name all seven of them?

11

◀ **3** How is a fossil made?

15

▼ **4** What happens when a volcano erupts?

18

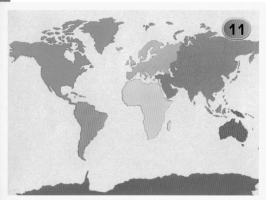
22

◀ **5** Can you explain how each of these lakes has been formed?

▼ **6** Where would you find stalactites and stalagmites? What is the difference between them?

25

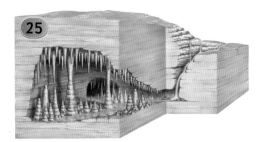

▼ **7** What are these grasslands called? How many other kinds of grassland can you name?

29

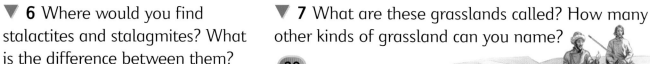

◀ **8** Which kind of tree keeps its leaves all year round? Which kind loses its leaves in winter?

31

◀ **9** Which animals have a long sleep in winter? What is this sleep called?

34

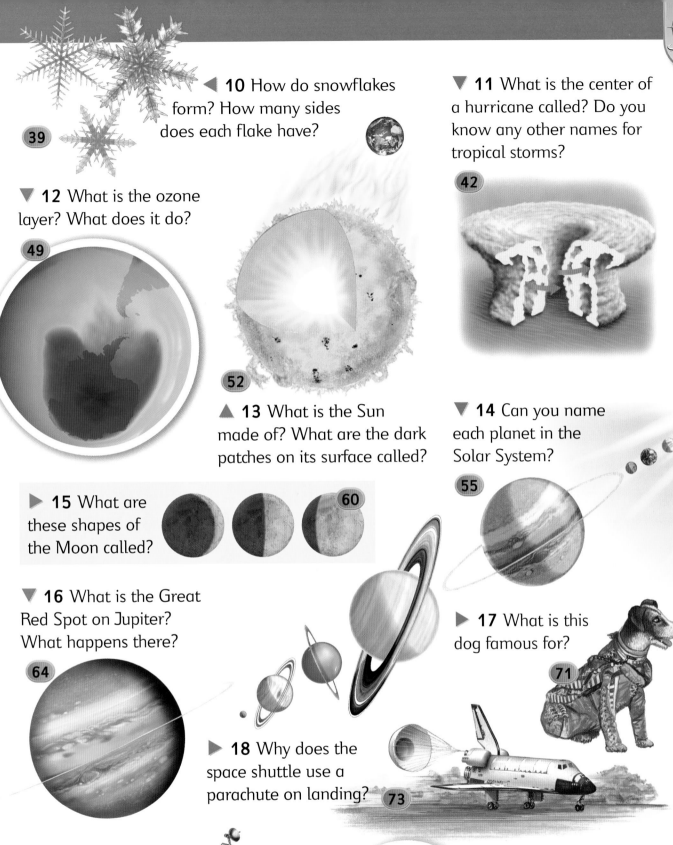

10 How do snowflakes form? How many sides does each flake have?

39

11 What is the center of a hurricane called? Do you know any other names for tropical storms?

42

12 What is the ozone layer? What does it do?

49

52

13 What is the Sun made of? What are the dark patches on its surface called?

14 Can you name each planet in the Solar System?

55

15 What are these shapes of the Moon called?

60

16 What is the Great Red Spot on Jupiter? What happens there?

64

17 What is this dog famous for?

71

18 Why does the space shuttle use a parachute on landing?

73

19 What is this giant telescope called? Where is it?

85

87

20 What kind of galaxy is this? Can you name our own galaxy?

Index

This index is an alphabetical list of subjects contained within the pages of your book. Some of the subjects have another alphabetical list underneath them. These are called sub-entries, and they tell you what sort of information you can find about the main subject. The page numbers where you will find the most information are printed in **bold**.

A

aboriginal people ⑥ **34**
Aconcagua mountain ⑥ **20**
actors ④ **86–87**, ⑤ 65
adults ⑤ **76–77**, 88
Africa ⑥ 11, **30–31**, **32–33**
  animals ③ 9, 74, 79, 80, ⑥ 10, 11
  crafts ④ 64
  desert people ④ **34**, **35**
  grasslands ③ 74, ④ 38
  rain forests ③ 79, 80, ④ 41
  savannahs ① 28
air ② 20, **22**
  atmosphere ① **50**
  breathing ⑤ 25
  transportation ② **70–71**, **74–75**
  weather ① 32
Alaska ④ 9, ⑥ **14**, 38
Alexandria Lighthouse ④ 14
algae ③ **12–13**
alligators ③ **56**
alphabets ④ **52–53**
Alps mountains ① 20–21, ③ 82
Amazon ① **30**, ③ 81, ⑥ **18**, 20
ammonites ① **14–15**
amphibians ③ **40**, **54–55**
Amundsen, Roald ④ **37**
ancient Egypt ① 53, ④ **14**, **15**, **16–17**, 54, ⑥ 32
  hieroglyphs ④ 52
ancient Greece ④ **14**, **15**, **18–19**
Andes mountains ⑥ 18, 19, 20, 21
Angel Falls ⑥ **21**
animals ① 9, ② 10–11, ③ 8–9, **38–39**, **78–79**
  communication ⑤ 67
  hibernation ① 34
  plant-eaters ③ **36–37**
  skeletons ③ **40**

Antarctica ① 11, 26, 49, ③ 86, ⑥ 11, 18, 38, **41**
  people ④ 36
anteater ③ **64**, ⑤ 53
ants ③ **44**, 79
Arab people ④ **24–25**, **54**, ⑥ 30
Arctic Ocean ① 12, ③ 86, ⑥ 14, 22, 26, 38, **40**
Argentina ① 28, ⑥ **18–19**, 20
Arizona ① 68, ⑥ 17
armadillo ③ **64**
arteries ⑤ **28–29**, 38–39
artists ④ 79, **80–81**
Asia ① 11, ⑥ 22, **26–27**, **28–29**
  animals ③ 80, 85
  early people ④ 10, 73
  grasslands ① **28–29**, ④ 38
asteroids ① 54, 55, 57, **68–69**
astronauts ① **50–51**, **70–71**, ④ 31
  on the Moon ① **74–75**, 77
Atacama desert ⑥ 18
Athens, Greece ⑥ 25
Atlantic Ocean ① 12, ⑥ 18
atoms ② **16–17**
Australia ③ 19, ④ 46, 64, ⑥ 11, **34–35**, 36
  animals ③ 75, 77, 85
autumn ① **34–35**, ③ 10–11
Aztec people ① 53

B

babies ⑤ 69, **70–71**, 88
  birth ⑤ **72–73**
  mammals ③ **62–63**
  reflexes ⑤ **46**
backbone ③ 39, ⑤ 18, 42, 43
Baffin Island ⑥ 16
balance ⑤ **51**
ballet dancing ⑤ **86**, ⑥ **25**
Bangkok, Thailand ⑥ **11**
bats ① 34, ② 39, ③ **64**

batteries ② **36–37**
Bavaria ⑥ 23
beaks ③ **60**
bears ① 34, ③ 83
Bedouin people ⑥ **28**
beetles ③ 39, **42–43**, 72
Beijing, China ④ 9
Benin ⑥ 33
Berber people ⑥ **33**
birds ③ **40**, 58–59, **60–61**
  Arctic terns ⑥ **39**
  colors ② 43
  forest ③ 76, 80
  hornbills ③ 80
  kiwi ⑥ **35**
  nesting ③ 10, 22
  of prey ③ **60**, 80, ⑥ **19**
  puffin ⑥ 22
  seashore ③ 68
birth ⑤ **72–73**
bison ③ 75, ④ 39
blood ⑤ 27, 28–29, **30–31**, 39
blood vessels ⑤ 15, 21, **28–29**, 31
  skin ⑤ 16
boats ② **66–67**, **68–69**
Bolivia ⑥ 19, **20**
bones ⑤ 15, **18–19**, **30**
  animals ② 10, ③ 40
  ear ⑤ 50
books ④ **78–79**
Braille ⑤ **56**
brain ⑤ 15, 20, **40–41**, 44
  emotions ⑤ 61
  nerves ⑤ 42–43
  reflexes ⑤ 46
  senses ⑤ 48, 50, 52
  sleep ⑤ 68
  thinking ⑤ **58–59**
Brazil ① 30, ④ 51, **54**, ⑥ 18, 19
breathing ① 31, ⑤ **24–25**
  baby ⑤ 72
  problems ⑤ 27
  sleep ⑤ 68
  sneezes ⑤ 26
bridges ② **82–83**

broad-leaved trees ③ **20–21**, 76
Buddhists ④ 55, **69**
Buenos Aires, Argentina ⑥ **18**, **19**
buildings ② 52, **86–87**
butterflies ③ **44**, 76–77, ⑥ 37

C

cactus ① **26–27**, ③ 27, 84, ⑥ 14, 15
Caesar, Julius ④ **22**
Cairo, Egypt ⑥ **31**, 32
camels ③ 85, ④ **34–35**, ⑥ 31
Canada ④ 39, 59, ⑥ 14–15, 16–17, 38
carbon dioxide ① 19, ② **20–21**
  plants ① **30–31**, ③ 24
Caribbean Islands ④ **26**, 82, **87**, ⑥ 14
carnivals ④ **71**, ⑥ **19**, **22**
carnivores ③ **36–37**
cars ② **62–63**, 82–83
  engines ② 28, 59
  factories ② **84–85**, ④ **64–65**
Caspian Sea ① **22**
caterpillar ③ **44**
cats ② 39, ③ **63**, ⑤ 67
Caucasus mountains ⑥ 22
caves ① **24–25**
cells ⑤ **30–31**, 70
Central America ④ **12**, ⑥ 14, 18
Chicago, USA ② 86
Chichén Itzá, Mexico ⑥ **16**
Chile ⑥ 18
China ④ 9, ⑥ 26, 29
  empires ④ 24
  Great Wall of ⑥ **29**
  New Year ④ **70**
  people ④ 10, 45, ⑤ 10
chipmunks ① 34, ③ 22
Christ ④ **68**, 70
Christians ④ **24**, 70, 83, ⑥ **27**
Christmas ④ 68, 69, **70–71**

circuits (2) **36**
cities (4) **50–51**, (5) 9, (6) **10**, 26, 31
civilizations, early (4) **10**, **16**, (6) 19
climate (1) **32–33**, (3) 82, (6) **12–13**, 34
clouds (1) 32–33, 40–41
 water cycle (1) 13, **38–39**, (2) 25
coal (1) 31, **46**, (2) **28–29**, 30
coast erosion (1) **24**, (6) 34
Colorado river (1) **44**, (6) 17
colors (2) **42–43**, (4) 80–81
Columbus, Christopher (4) **26**
comets (1) 54–55, **68–69**
communication (2) **76–77**, **78–79**, **80–81**, (4) 53
 animals (5) 67
 social (5) **62–63**, 67
computers (2) **78–79**
 designers (2) 55
 future (2) **88–89**
 games (4) 72
 robots (2) 85
conduction (2) **26**
conifer trees (1) **30–31**, (3) **20–21**, 76
conservation (3) **88–89**
constellations (1) **84–85**, 87
continents (1) **10–11**, (6) **10**, 14–15, 26, 30
convection (2) **26**
Copernicus (2) **8**, (4) **27**
coral reefs (6) **34–35**
core (Earth) (1) **58–59**
coyote (1) 26
crabs (3) **69**, (5) 45
cranes (2) **52–53**
Crete (2) **72–73**, (4) **18–19**
crocodiles (3) **56**
crust (Earth) (1) **58–59**
currency (4) **56–57**
Czech Republic (6) 23

D

dance (5) **86**, (6) **25**, 33
da Vinci, Leonardo (4) **27**
deserts (1) 10, (6) **13**
 Africa (6) 30–31
 animals and plants (1) 8, **26–27**, (3) **84–85**
 Asia (6) 26
 Australia (6) **34**
 North America (6) 14, 15
 people (4) **34–35**
design (2) **54–55**, (4) 59, 78
digestive system (5) **34–35**, 68
dinosaurs (2) 11
discoveries (4) **26–27**
diseases (5) **17**

dissolving (2) **18–19**
dolphins (3) **63**, 66–67, (5) 63
dragonfly (3) 72
dreams (5) 69
duck-billed platypus (3) **62**, (5) 73

E

eagle (6) 15
ears (2) **44**, (5) 22, **50–51**, 68
Earth (1) **58–59**
 life on (1) **8–9**
 magnetic (2) 35
 planet (1) **50–51**, **54–55**, **56**, **62–63**
 time (4) 8, 9
earthquake (1) **16–17**, (5) 88
Ecuador (4) 64
Egypt (5) 73, (6) 31, 32
 ancient (1) 53, (4) **14–15**, **16–17**, 52, 54
 gods (4) 16
Eiffel Tower (6) **25**
electrical nerve signals (5) **42**
electricity (1) 32, 43, (2) **32**, **36–37**, 39
 lightning (1) 40–41
elephant (3) **36**, **89**, (5) 32, (6) **32**
emotions (5) **60–61**
energy (1) 17, (2) **28–29**, **30–31**, 60
 food (5) **36–37**
 Sun (1) **32**, 52
engineers (4) **60**, 62
engines (2) **58–59**, 65, 66
England (1) 45, (4) 9, (6) 22, 24
Equator (1) **34–35**, (6) 30
erosion (1) **24–25**
Euphrates river (4) 10
Europe (1) 11, 20–21, (3) 77, (6) 8, **22–23**, **24–25**
 discoveries (4) **26–27**
 empires (4) **24–25**
 grassland people (4) 38
evergreen trees (1) **30–31**, (3) **20–21**, (6) 14
explorers (2) 66, (4) 26–27, **62**
eyes (2) **40**, (3) 42–43, (5) 42, **48–49**, 83,

F

facial expressions (4) 53, (5) **64–65**
factories (2) **84–85**, (4) **28–29**, **64–65**
family (4) 70, (5) 10–11, **12–13**, 62
farmers (4) 10, **60–61**

farming (1) **46**
farmland (1) 28, (6) 22
feathers (3) 40, **58–59**
feelings (5) **60–61**, 62, 64, 66
ferns (3) **14–15**
festivals (4) **70–71**, (6) 33, 35
Finland (4) 60, (6) 24
firefighters (4) **66–67**
fish (2) 19, (3) **40**, **50–51**, 52–53, 70–71
fishermen (4) **44**, **62–63**
fishing (1) **46**
flags (6) 42–43
Fleming, Alexander (2) **8**
flowers (2) 43, (3) 25, **28–29**, 30, (6) **29**
flowering plants (3) 13, **16–17**, 82
fly (3) 45, 73
food (5) **84**, (6) **23**, 27
 energy (2) **28–29**, 60, (5) **36–37**
 plants (3) **26–27**, **36–37**
food chain (2) 11, (3) 36
football (4) **74–75**, (6) 15
forces (2) **34**, **46–47**
forests (1) 8, 10, **30–31**
 Asia (6) 26
 North America (6) 14
fossils (1) **14–15**
France (4) **23**, 50, (6) 10, 11, 25
French Revolution (4) **29**
frogs (3) 22, **54–55**, 73, 79, (4) 41
fruits (3) 26, **30–31**
fungi (3) **34–35**

G

Gagarin, Yuri (1) **70–71**
galaxies (1) **86–87**, 88, 89
Galileo (1) 66
games (4) **72–73**
Ganges river (4) 69
gas (fuel) (1) 31, **46**, (2) **21**, **28–29**, 30
gases (1) 19, **48**, (2) **20–21**
gears (2) **50–51**
Germany (6) 23
germs (5) 16, 86
geysers (1) **44**, (2) 20
Giant's Causeway (1) **45**
giraffe (6) **31**
glands (5) **16–17**
glass (1) **49**, (2) 12
gliders (2) **74–75**
goats (3) 83, (4) 34
Gobi desert (3) 85
gods (4) **68**
Grand Canyon (1) **44–45**, (6) **17**

grasshopper (3) 37, (5) 51
grasslands (1) **28–29**, (3) **74–75**
 Africa (6) 30, 32
 Asia (6) 26
 Australia (6) 34
 North America (6) 14
 people (4) **38–39**
 South America (6) 18
gravity (2) 9, 24, **46–47**, 60
Great Rift Valley (6) 30
Great Wall of China (6) **29**
Greece (4) 33, (6) 25
 ancient (4) **14–15**, **16–17**, **76**
Greenland (6) 14–15, 16, 38–39
growing (5) **74–75**, **78–79**

H

hair (3) 40, **62–63**, (5) **16–17**
 growing old (5) 80
 washing (5) 87
hamsters (3) 74
hands (4) 53, (5) **78–79**
Hawaii (1) 39
hearing (2) **44**, (5) **50–51**, 80
heart (5) 15, 24, **28–29**
 emotions (5) 61
 sleep (5) 68
heat (2) **26–27**, 28
helicopters (2) **70**, (3) 59
herbivores (3) **36–37**
Herschel, William (1) **66**
hibernation (1) **34**
hiccups (5) **26–27**, 46
Hillary, Edmund (1) **21**
Himalaya mountains (4) 43, (6) **26**, 29
Hindus (4) **69**, **71**
hobbies (4) **72–73**
holidays (4) 70
Homer (4) **19**
Hong Kong (4) 45
horses (3) **62**, (5) 32
horsetails (3) **15**
house plants (3) **27**
hovercraft (2) 22, 68
human beings (5) **8–9**
hummingbirds (3) **58–59**, 60
hunter-gatherers (4) 10
hunters (6) 21
hurricanes (1) 40, **42–43**

I

ice (1) 10, 39, (2) 24
 deserts (1) 8, **26**, (3) 86
 mountains (6) 12
 polar regions (6) 38–39
icebergs (1) **44**, (2) 24
ice hockey (5) **89**, (6) 17
igneous rocks (1) **14**

immunization ⑤ 83
Inca people ⑥ **19**
India ① 45, ⑥ 26
  British rule ④ **29**
  clothes ④ **54**
  empires ④ 24
  games ④ 72
  tea picking ④ 60
Indian Ocean ① 12, ⑥ 26,
  34
Indonesia ④ 26, 46, 82
industry ④ **28–29**
insect-eating plants ③ **32–33**
insects ③ 22, **42–43**, **44–45**
  and flowers ③ 16, **28–29**
internet ② **78–79**, ④ **30**,
  46, ⑤ 81
Inuit people ④ **54**,
  ⑥ **14–15**, 39
inventions ④ 26–27, **30–31**
invertebrate animals ② **10**,
  ③ **38–39**
Iraq ④ 10
islands ① **10–11**, 12,
  ⑥ **34–35**
Israel ⑥ 27
Italy ④ 45, ⑥ 22–23, 24

J
Japan ① 16, ⑥ 26
  clothes ④ **54**
  empires ④ **25**
  food ④ **33**
jellyfish ③ 38, 66–67
Jerusalem, Israel ⑥ **27**
Jews ④ **68**, ⑥ 27
joints ⑤ 22, 80
Jupiter (planet) ① **55**,
  56–57, **64–65**, 82, 83,
  ③ 9

K
K2 mountain ① **45**
Kalahari desert ④ **35**
kangaroo ② 47, ③ **63**, 75,
  ⑥ **36**
kidneys ⑤ **38–39**, 68
kingfisher ③ 71
knights ④ 24

L
Lake Ontario ⑥ 14
lakes ① **22–23**, ④ 44
Lake Titicaca ⑥ **20**
languages ④ **52–53**
lava ① **18–19**, ② 17, ④ 42
leaves ③ **12–13**, **18–19**, 24
  trees ① **30–31**, ③ 20–21
leech ③ 70
lenses ② 9, 40, ⑤ 48
leopard, snow ⑥ **28**
levers ② **48–49**

lifeboat ④ **66**
light ② **38–39**, **40–41**
  colors ① 53, ② 42
  energy ② 28
  seeing ⑤ 48
  Sun ① **52–53**
lightning ① **40–41**,
  ② **32–33**
lion ① **29**, ③ **37**, 89, ⑤ 33,
  67, ⑥ **11**
liquids ② **18–19**
liver ⑤ 15, **35**
liverworts ③ **15**
lizards ③ **56–57**, 85, ⑤ 67
llamas ⑥ **21**
locust ③ 45
London, England ④ 9, ⑥ 22
lungs ⑤ 15, **24–25**, 28–29,
  38
  baby ⑤ 72
  sneezes and hiccups ⑤ 26

M
machines ② **56–57**, **86–87**
  engines ② 58
  factories ② 84, ④ **28**
  motors ② 60
  simple ② **48–49**
Machu Picchu, Peru ⑥ **19**
Madagascar ① 11
magnets ② **34–35**, 53, 61, 64
mammals ③ **40**, **62–63**, **64**,
  ⑤ **73**
mantle (Earth) ① **58–59**
Maori people ⑥ **37**
maps ② **83**, ⑥ **8–9**, **10**
Marianas Trench ① **12**
markets ④ 56, 58
Mars ① 54–55, 56, **62–63**,
  83
marsupials ③ **62–63**
Masai people ④ **38**, ⑥ **30**
materials ② **12–13**, **14**,
  16–17
Mausoleum ④ **15**
Mayan people ④ **13**, ⑥ **16**
Mbuti people ④ **41**
Mecca ④ 68
medicine ② 8, ③ 35,
  ④ **30–31**
Mediterranean Sea ⑥ 22
memory ⑤ **58–59**
Mercury ① **55**, 56, **62–63**
  spacecraft ① 83
metamorphic rocks ① **14**
Mexico ① 53, ⑥ **14–15**, 16
  empires ④ 24
  first people ④ **12–13**
  food ④ 33
microphone ② 77
microscope ② **9**, 40–41,
  ③ 35, ⑤ 17

Middle Ages ④ **25**, ⑥ 24
Middle East ④ **11**, 24
minerals ③ 13, 25, 32,
  ⑤ 35, 36, 84
miners ④ **60–61**
mistletoe ③ **33**
mites ③ 39, **48–49**
mollusks ③ **69**
money ④ **56–57**
Mongolian people ④ **39**
monkey ③ **79**
Mont-Saint-Michel ⑥ **11**
Moon ① **58–59**, **60–61**
  landing ① 59, **74–75**,
  ④ **31**, ⑤ 81
moons ① 54, 63, 67, ③ 9
Morocco ⑥ 33
Moscow, Russia ⑥ 23, 25
mosquitoes ③ **45**
mosses ③ **14–15**, 70
motors ② **60–61**, 66
Mount Everest ① **21**,
  ⑥ **29**
Mount Kilimanjaro ⑥ **30**,
  32
Mount Mckinley ⑥ **14**
Mount Rushmore ⑥ **16**
mountains ① 8, 10, **20–21**,
  ③ 82
  Africa ⑥ 30
  Asia ⑥ 26
  climate ⑥ 12
  Europe ⑥ 23
  maps ⑥ 8
  people ④ **42–43**
  rescue ④ **66–67**
  volcanoes ① 18
mouth ⑤ 24, 32, 33
  facial expressions ⑤ 65
  speaking ⑤ 67
movement ② 28, **46–47**,
  60–61, ⑤ 20
movies ④ **88**
Muhammad ④ **68**
muscles ② 46, 60, ⑤ 15,
  20–21, **22–23**, 44
  birth ⑤ 72
  facial expressions ⑤ 65
  fish ③ **50–51**
  heart ⑤ 28
  reflexes ⑤ 46
  shivering ⑤ 17
  sleep ⑤ 68
  speaking ⑤ 66
music ④ **82–83**, 84
Muslims ④ **24**, **68**, 70,
  ⑥ **27**

N
nails (skin) ⑤ **17**
Namib desert ① **44**
Namibian clothes ④ **54**

Native American people
  ① 61, ④ **39**, ⑥ **15**
Nebuchadnezzar, King
  ④ **14–15**
Nefertiti, Queen ④ **17**
Nepal ⑥ 29
Neptune (planet) ① 54, 56,
  66–67, 83
nerves ⑤ 15, **40–41**, **42–43**,
  44
  reflexes ⑤ 46
  seeing ⑤ 48
Netherlands ④ 71, ⑥ 23
Newfoundland ⑥ 16
Newton, Isaac ② **9**
newts ③ **54–55**
New Year festival ④ **70**
New York City, USA ④ **51**,
  ⑥ 10, 16
New Zealand ④ 47, 60,
  ⑥ **34–35**, 37
Nigeria ① 13, ④ 56
Nile river ① **22**, ④ **16–17**,
  ⑥ 31
nitrogen ① **50**, ② 20
nocturnal animals ② **39**
Norgay, Tensing ① **21**
Normandy, France ⑥ 11
North America ① 11,
  ⑥ **14–15**, **16–17**
  empires ④ 24
  grasslands ④ 38
  people ④ 12, ⑤ 69
  plants and animals ③ 12,
  75
  prairies ① 28
Northern Ireland ① 45
northern lights ④ **36**
North Pole ② 24, 35, ⑥ **38**
  magnetism ② 35
  ozone hole ① 49
  people ④ **36–37**
Norway ⑥ 24
nose ⑤ 24, **52–53**
  sneezes ⑤ 26
nutrients ⑤ **34–35**, **36**

O
Oceania ① 11, ⑥ **34–35**
oceans ① 9, **12–13**, 59,
  ② 24, ⑥ **10**, ③ **66–67**
octopus ③ 66–67
Odysseus ① **43**, ② **66–67**
oil (fuel) ① 31, **46**,
  ② **28–29**, 30, 69
  spills ① **48**
Olmec people ④ **13**
Olympic Games ④ **76**
omnivores ③ **36–37**
orbits ① **56–57**, 58,
  60
Orinoco river ③ 81